CHECKMATES FOR WINNING CHESS PLAYERS

ABOUT THE AUTHOR

Bill Robertie is the world's best backgammon player and the only two-time winner of the Monte Carlo World Championships. Robertie is the author of seven backgammon books and the co-publisher of *Inside Backgammon*, the leading backgammon magazine. He also is a chess master, winner of the U.S. Speed Chess Championship, and the author of six chess books. Robertie's club and tournament winnings have allowed him to travel the world in style. He currently makes his home in Arlington, Massachusetts.

BACKGAMMON AND CHESS BOOKS BY BILL ROBERTIE

501 Essential Backgammon Problems
Backgammon for Winners
Backgammon for Serious Players
Advanced Backgammon Volume 1: Positional Play
Advanced Backgammon Volume 2: Technical Play
Lee Genud vs. Joe Dwek
Reno 1986
Beginning Chess Play
Checkmates for Winning Chess Players
Winning Chess Tactics
Winning Chess Openings
Basic Endgame Strategy: Kings, Pawns, & Minor Pieces
Basic Endgame Strategy: Queens and Rooks
How to Win Chess Endgames

CHECKMATES FOR WINNING CHESS PLAYERS

BILL ROBERTIE

CARDOZA PUBLISHING

Cardoza Publishing is the foremost gaming publisher in the world with a library of more than 200 up-to-date and easy-to-read books and strategies. These authoritative works are written by the top experts in their fields and with more than 10,000,000 books in print, represent the best-selling and most popular gaming books anywhere.

2018 EDITION
2nd Printing

Formerly titled Master Checkmate Strategy

ISBN 13: 978-1-58042-370-0

CARDOZA PUBLISHING
P.O. Box 98115, Las Vegas, NV 89193
Toll-Free Phone (800)577-WINS
email: cardozabooks@aol.com
www.cardozabooks.com

TABLE OF CONTENTS

1

INTRODUCTION

There are two ways to win a chess game.

One way is solid, steady, and unspectacular. You gradually outplay your opponent, piling small advantage on top of small advantage. You win a little material along the way, and finally score a win in the endgame. The spectators greet your achievement with polite but modest applause.

The other way is harder but much more satisfying. You activate your pieces early in the game, generating threats that push your opponent back to the wall. You blast through the pawns and pieces guarding his King with a brilliant sacrifice, and crown your achievement with an amazing checkmate, seemingly conjured out of thin air. The spectators scream themselves hoarse as they carry you from the room on their shoulders.

In this book I'm going to show you the secrets of winning checkmating attacks. You'll learn how to spot the conditions that make an attack possible, how to break through your opponent's defenses, and how to push his King off to the side of the board. You'll also learn the basic checkmating patterns that can turn apparently difficult attacks into easy and exciting wins. With this knowledge, you'll win more often, and enjoy the game a lot more.

Now let's get started!

2

CHESS NOTATION

Chess notation is a simplified way of recording the moves in a chess game. By learning chess notation, you'll be able to follow the games and explanations in this or any other chess book. It's really quite easy. Here's how it works.

Chess notation starts by putting a coordinate grid over the chessboard. Take a look at the diagram below.

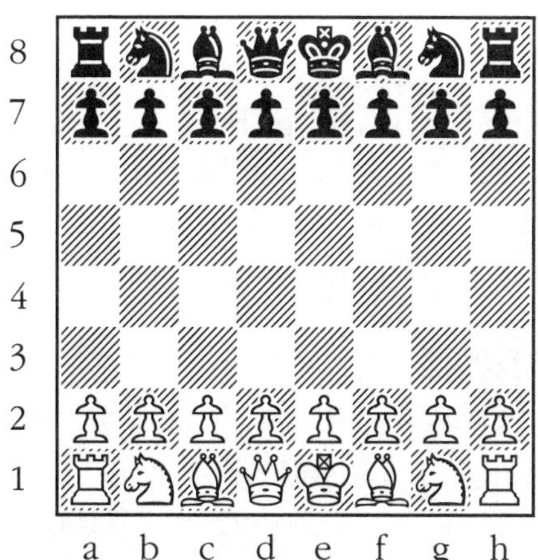

Diagram 1: The Notation System.

THE NOTATION SYSTEM

The horizontal rows, or **ranks**, are numbered from 1 to 8. White's first row, the rank containing the White pieces, is number 1. The rank with Black's pieces is now number 8. The vertical rows, or **files**, are lettered "a" through "h", with "a" starting on White's left and "h" on White's right.

This grid system lets us refer to any square on the board by a unique name. White's King is currently sitting on the square "e1". Black's Queen is on square "d8", and so on. In addition to the grid system, we have abbreviations for each of the pieces. Here they are:

ABBREVIATIONS FOR THE PIECES	
King	K
Queen	Q
Rook	R
Bishop	B
Knight	N
Pawn	-

To indicate a move, we write down the piece that moved, and the starting and ending squares of the move. However, if a pawn is moving, we don't need to write anything more than the starting and ending squares. We use a dash to separate the starting and ending squares, and an "x" if the move was a capture.

SPECIAL NOTATIONS

Certain moves in chess have their own special notation:

- Castling King-side is denoted by "0-0".
  Castling Queen-side is denoted by "0-0-0".
- When promoting a pawn, indicate the promoted piece in parentheses: for instance, "a7-a8(Q)" says that white moved a pawn to the a8 square and promoted it to a Queen.
- Capturing en passant is denoted by "ep" after the move; for instance, "d5xc6 ep" shows a pawn capturing en passant on the c6 square.

We use exclamation points and question marks to comment on the ingenuity or effectiveness of moves. Here's what they mean:

ANNOTATION COMMENTS

! means a good move.
!! means a brilliant, completely unexpected move.
? means an error.
?? means a gross blunder, probably losing the game.

3

PLAYING FOR CHECKMATE

Most chess games are won in a slow and steady fashion. You outmaneuver your opponent in the opening, gaining a slight advantage in mobility. Then, using the techniques described in my book, *Winning Chess Tactics*, you use tactical play to win some material – perhaps a piece or even just a pawn or two. Playing carefully, you exchange pieces at every opportunity until you reach the endgame where your extra material has more significance. You use your extra material to march your pawns up the board where one becomes a Queen. With this overwhelming material advantage, you herd your opponent's King into a corner and administer a brutal but effective checkmate.

This approach is like a boxer who wins a match on points, or a tennis player who beats you with steady groundstrokes from the baseline. It's professional, it's workmanlike, it gets the job done with a minimum of flair and risk.

But there's another approach to winning at chess – and it's fast, sharp, and deadly. It's the checkmating attack, equivalent to a knockout punch in boxing or a serve and volley game in tennis.

Sometimes your opponent, pursuing his own plans to win, will leave the lines to his King a little bit exposed. If he's trying for an advantage on the other side of the board, he may pull some of his defensive pieces away from his King. That can open up lines of attack for you – if you know how to exploit them. By moving your own pieces to the attack, and taking advantage of weaknesses, you may be able to end the game with a direct checkmate attack in the middle game or even right in the opening! A checkmating attack isn't just flashy or exciting. If your opponent has left you the opportunity, then you must take it. Remember that a lot can go wrong when you try to nurse a small advantage of an extra pawn or two through a long game. Your opponent will have many opportunities to set traps and put up resistance. But when you checkmate him, he's done.

THE PRECONDITIONS FOR A MATING ATTACK

Not every position is suitable for a mating attack. Trying to force a mating attack where the conditions aren't right just won't work. Your attack will be beaten back, usually with loss of material in the process. A key part of being a good attacking player is learning to recognize when an attack is possible, and only attacking when the conditions are right.

What makes a successful attack possible? In general, two conditions need to be met:

- You need an advantage in space, particularly in the area of the board where your opponent's King is located.
- You must have more pieces available for attack than your opponent has for defense.

The second condition doesn't mean you have to be ahead in material; it just means you need more pieces around your opponent's King than he can muster for defense. (If your opponent's defensive pieces are poorly placed or unable to cooperate, you may not even need a preponderance of material.)

Now let's take a look at a couple of checkmating attacks, while paying attention to how these two conditions are satisfied.

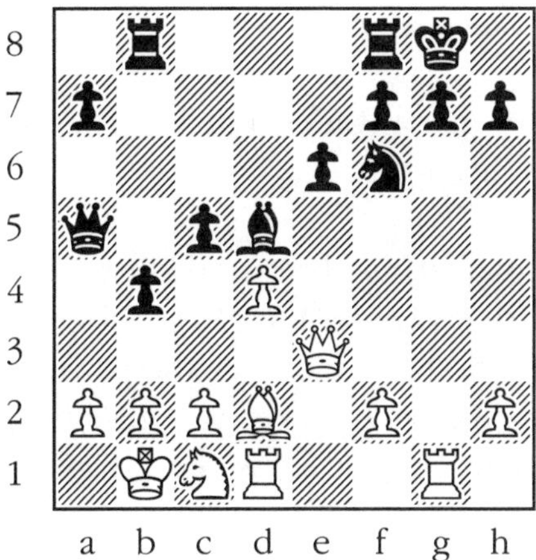

Diagram 2: White on move.

In Diagram 2, White is one pawn down. However, he's not unhappy. The pawn that he's missing is the one that started the game on g2, and with that pawn out of the way, White's Rooks have an open line of attack along the g-file to Black's King.

Let's take a look at our preconditions and see how they apply to this position. Does White have an advantage in space in the area around Black's King? Absolutely. White's pieces control the whole open area on the King-side, and they can move about freely. Black's pieces control space on the Queen-side, around the White King.

How about an advantage in material around the Black King?

Again, White has a solid edge in this area. His Rooks can use the g-file, which aims right at the Black King. White's Queen can move to g5, e5, or h6, while the White Bishop is aimed at the Black squares g5 and h6. The only White piece that couldn't participate in an attack is the White Knight back on c1. It's too far away from the scene of the action, and since Knights move slowly, it would take the Knight at least three turns to reach the area around the Black King.

Black has a Knight and a Rook for defense, but his other pieces are busy on the Queen-side.

How does White exploit his advantage in firepower? Let's watch. He starts with the explosive **1 Rg1xg7 check!!** The Rook sacrifices itself to blast away one of the pawns defending the King. (As it happens, this is a key pawn, the linchpin of Black's defenses.) Black captures the Rook, **1 ... Kg8xg7**.

Now White swoops in with **2 Qe3-g5 check!** The Queen attacks the King and simultaneously threatens the Knight. Black's reply is forced: **2 ... Kg7-h8.**

The King had to give up its defense of the Knight, so White picks it off: **3 Qg5xf6 check.** Black's reply is again forced. He plays **3 ... Kh8-g8**.

White finally puts Black out of his misery with **4 Rd1-g1 check.** After Black interposes the Bishop on g2, White will capture it, announcing checkmate at the same time.

THE THREE KEY ATTACKING TECHNIQUES

Conducting a successful mating attack requires mastering three key attacking skills. The previous problem illustrated all three techniques in action. Let's take a look at them.

Technique #1
Strip away the pawns in front of the enemy King.

After castling on the King-side, the three pawns in front of the King constitute a powerful defensive barrier. As long as these pawns are securely in place, it's very hard to get at the enemy

King. Many checkmating combinations begin with the sacrifice of a Bishop, Knight, or Rook to blast through the array of pawns and expose the enemy King.

From the defender's point of view, the best defensive structure is to have the pawns in front of the King on their original squares. This offers two advantages. First, since the pawns haven't yet moved, they are all free to move as necessary to respond to any particular threat. (Once the pawns start moving, their freedom of future movement gets limited quickly.) Second, pawns on their original squares are as far away as possible from the enemy pieces. This makes the logistics of attacking the pawns as difficult as it can be.

Technique #2
Use the power of check to mobilize your pieces.

The cry of "check" forces your opponent to ignore everything else and move the King to safety. While he's moving his King, he can't mobilize his other pieces into defensive positions. In the previous problem, Black would have liked to move his Queen back into the action, but he couldn't. White operated with checks every move, and Black was forced to keep shuffling his King until the final blow fell.

As we'll see in this book, many successful mating attacks follow this exact pattern: an initial sacrifice to strip away defenses, a series of forcing checks driving the King off to the side of the board or into a corner, followed by a checkmate.

Technique #3
Calculate the follow-up accurately.

Sacrificing pieces around your opponent's King is easy. The hard part is calculating the follow-up. In almost all cases, you have to be able to see your way through to checkmate before you sacrifice any pieces. After all, if you give up a Rook for a pawn, get a check or two, and then discover that there's no checkmate in the position, you're going to lose. You'd have been much better off keeping your Rook and playing a slower game where you had a chance to win.

In this book we'll show you some ways to make calculating easier. Above all, you want to look for forcing moves: checks which leave your opponent only one square to run to, or threats which can be met in only one way. If you can find a series of forcing moves, it will be easier than you might think to imagine the positions several turns down the road. In our previous problem, note that every move after the initial Rook sacrifice left Black with only one legal reply. That made it easy for White to look three turns ahead and see the coming checkmate.

Let's try another example, and watch how Black uses our three techniques to win the game.

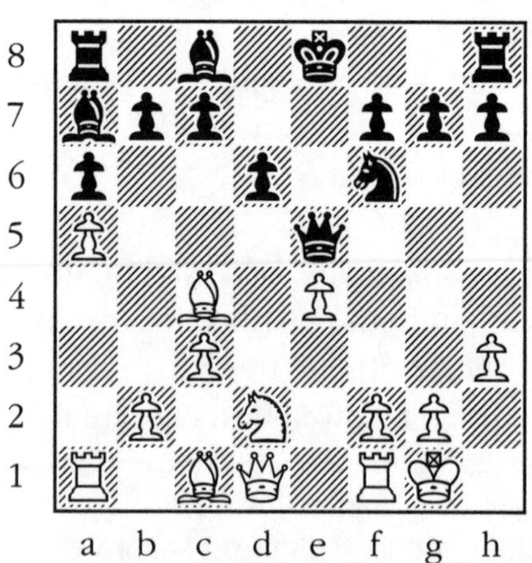

Diagram 3: Black to move

First let's check our two preconditions to see if an attack should be possible.

Does Black have an advantage in space around the enemy King? He certainly does. All the squares on the King-side of the board are easily accessible to the Black pieces.

Does Black have more pieces available for the attack than White does for the defense? Absolutely. Black's Queen and Knight are poised to attack, and both Black Bishops are aiming toward the enemy King down long diagonals. The Black-squared Bishop on a7 is aiming at the pawn on f2, while the White-squared Bishop on c8 is attacking the pawn on h3. White's King is only defended by the Rook on f1, and generally a Rook on f1 can't play much of a role, especially if the attack comes down the g- and h-files.

So the preconditions appear to be in place. But is a winning attack available? Let's watch as Black shows us the solution. He starts with an explosive sacrifice: **1 ... Bc8xh3!** This will have the effect of opening the g-file and loosening the defenses around White's King. White replies with **2 g2xh3**, capturing the Bishop.

Now Black plays the key move of his attacking combination: **2 ... Qe5-g3 check!!** This catches White completely by surprise. He had forgotten that since his pawn on f2 is pinned by the Black Bishop back on a7, it can't move to capture the Black Queen. (For a refresher course on pins, see our previous book in this series, *Winning Chess Tactics*.)

Since the pawn on f2 can't move, White doesn't have much choice. The only way to get the King out of check is to hide in the corner: **3 Kg1-h1**. Now Black snaps off the loose pawn on h3 with **3 ... Qg3xh3 check.** White meekly goes back where he came from, **4 Kh1-g1**.

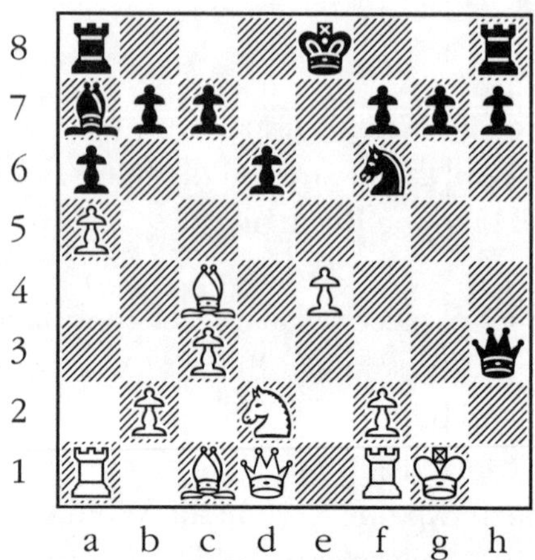

Diagram 4: Black to move

Black's done about all he can with the Queen and the Bishop. Now it's time to bring in the cavalry: **4 ... Nf6-g4!**

Although this move isn't a check, it's just as forcing as a check. By attacking the h2 square, Black now threatens Qh3-h2 checkmate. There's only one way White can deal with this threat. He has to guard the h2 square again, and the only piece available is the Knight. White plays **5 Nd2-f3.**

With Black's Knight now lending support from g4, Black has a way to force the checkmate. He starts off with **5 ... Qh3-g3 check**, (again relying on the pin), and White has to go back in the corner, **6 Kg1-h1**. Now Black finishes him off with **6 ... Ba7xf2!**

Take a look at the new position:

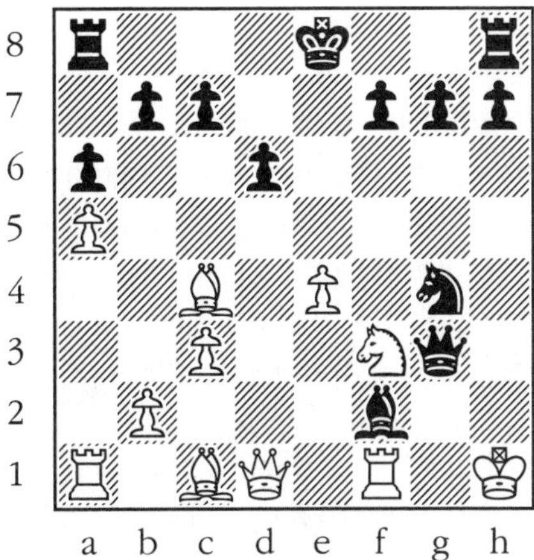

Diagram 5: White to move

The Bishop on f2 guards the g1 square, preventing the White King from moving there. As a result, Black threatens to play Qg3-h3, checkmate! White is helpless. If he captures the Bishop with Rf1xf2, Black plays Ng4xf2, checkmate. If he guards the h3 square with Nf3-g5, the Knight stops guarding the h2 square, so Black would play Qg3-h2 checkmate. White is helpless, so he gives up the game.

Notice how Black carefully applied the three winning techniques to this position. He began with a Bishop sacrifice which broke open the pawn position in front of White's King. Two moves later, both White's g-pawn and White's h-pawn were gone, and the King was totally exposed to the onslaught of the Black pieces.

Next, Black used checks and direct checkmating threats to bring his pieces close to White's King with gains of time. Black's second, third, fourth, and fifth moves all left White with only one move to either get out of check or avoid immediate checkmate. As a result, White was never able to mobilize the pieces sitting idly on the Queen-side.

In fact, the only Black move which didn't force White's hand was the initial sacrifice, **Bc8xh3**.

Note that White didn't have to capture the Bishop. He could have resigned himself to the loss of a pawn and played something like Qd1-f3. This would have guarded the crucial g2 and g3 squares, and prevented the slaughter which followed. Black would have then pulled back his Bishop, contenting himself with the profit of a single pawn and a very good position.

In many checkmating attacks, the defender has a chance to beat off the attack by submitting to a loss of material. If you see the attack is going to lead to a checkmate, that's your best course and perhaps the only way to salvage some winning chances. If you can't see a checkmate coming, then just take the material and see what happens.

Was Black able to calculate this attack all the way to the final position? We can't be sure. It's possible that Black only saw that he could quickly win two pawns for his Bishop while developing a strong position with many threats. In that case, his sacrifice was a calculated risk, but a perfectly reasonable one. If he saw his way through to the final checkmate, so much the better.

In these two examples, we've seen most of the basic ideas behind launching a checkmating attack. Now we're going to explore some of the typical mating patterns, one by one. In each chapter, we'll lay out the basic pattern and then take a look at a few examples, so you can see how the pros make it happen in practice.

4

ATTACKING THE F7 SQUARE

What's the weakest point in Black's defensive position at the beginning of the game? The f7 square. (For White it is f2.) That's because the pawn on that square is guarded only by the King. By contrast, the pawn on e7 is guarded by four pieces: the King, the Queen, the Bishop on f8, and the Knight on g8.

THE SCHOLAR'S MATE

With the f7 pawn guarded only by the King, a quick attack against that square can yield amazing results. Take a look at this quick game, known to chess players as the "Scholar's Mate":

1	**e2-e4**	**e7-e5**
2	**Bf1-c4**	**Bf8-c5**
3	**Qd1-f3**	**Nb8-c6??**
4	**Qf3xf7 mate**	

Diagram 6: Black has been checkmated!

This checkmate could have been easily avoided on Black's third move. He could have played Qd8-f6 or e7, defending the f7 pawn, or even more simply, Ng8-f6, developing a piece and blocking the Queen's attack. Still, try this attack in your own games. It's amazing how often this simple combination works, especially against inexperienced players.

TWO FEATURES TO LOOK FOR

Besides the general features of checkmating play that we discussed in the last chapter, there are two features to look for in early attacks against the f7 square.

The first is White's white-squared Bishop, which will be developed to the diagonal running from a2 to f7, probably at c4 or b3. White needs this Bishop to mount threats against f7 quickly. The second is the position of the Black King's Knight. If it's sitting on f6, an attack against f7 probably won't work. If it hasn't been developed, or if it's been chased away from f6, the f7 square may be vulnerable.

Now let's look at some more complicated attacks against the f7 square. If a game ends in checkmate in the very early stages, it's likely that the weakness of f7 (or f2 for White) was the culprit.

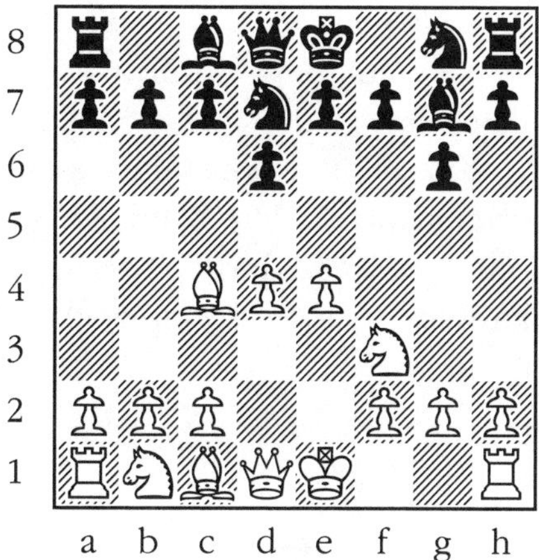

Diagram 7: White to move

In Diagram 7, we're just four moves into the game. White has developed nicely, with his pawns on d4 and e4 controlling the center, while his King's Knight is developed to its best square on f3. Most important, however, is his powerful King's Bishop, which at c4 is aimed at the weak Black pawn on f7. Black hasn't completely neglected his development, but his pieces have much less scope than White's. Most important, however, is the position of his King's Knight, still on its original square at g8.

When Black leaves that Knight undeveloped, he's always more vulnerable to an attack on the f7 square.

White sees the opportunity for an attack on f7 and immediately pounces. He starts with a sacrifice: **1 Bc4xf7 check!**

Black doesn't have a lot of choice. If he doesn't take the Bishop, White will be a pawn ahead with a strong attack anyway. So he plays **1 ... Ke8xf7.** Now White continues the attack with a forcing check. He plays **2 Nf3-g5 check!**

What can Black do? If he plays Kf7-f8, White will win the Queen with a Knight fork by Ng5-e6 check! If he plays instead Kf7-e8, he loses even more ignominiously: White traps the Queen with Ng5-e6, and the Black Queen can't move! So Black tries the only other square, **2 ... Kf7-f6**. But White finishes him off anyway, with **3 Qd1-f3 checkmate!** The Black King can't take the Knight, since it's guarded by the Bishop back on c1, and all the other escape squares are attacked by either the White Knight or the White Queen.

Let's look at another example:

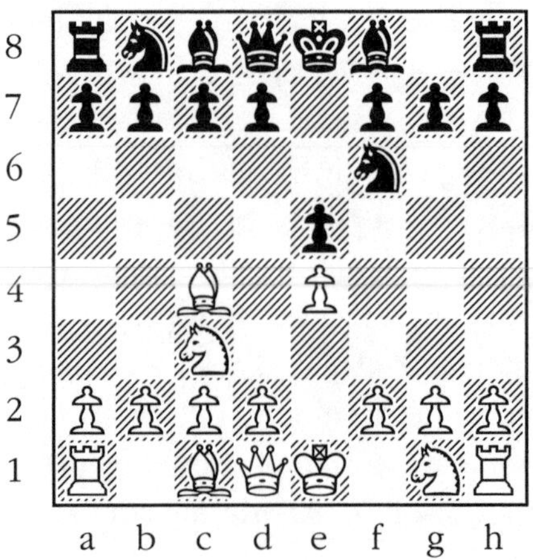

Diagram 8: Black on move

We're early in the opening, and White has developed his Bishop to the dangerous c4 square. Unlike the previous example, this time Black has developed his Knight to the good square f6. So far the game is in balance.

Black now sees a chance to gain an advantage in the center. He plays **1 ... Nf6xe4**. This appears to lose a Knight, but that's not the case. Black anticipates that White will play Nc3xe4, and he will follow with d7-d5!, forking the two White pieces.

Then White would play Bc4xd5, and Black would respond with Qd8xd5. The material would then be even (both sides would have lost a piece and a pawn), but Black would have a nice position in the center. Black's reasoning is correct as far as it goes, and his move is perfectly sound, if followed up properly. However, the play can get quite complicated, and Black must be prepared. In particular, White doesn't have to play Nc3xe4. Instead, he tries a different move: **2 Bc4xf7 check.**

Black didn't expect this! White has managed to trade pieces in a slightly different way, meanwhile exposing the Black King. Black plays **2 ... Ke8xf7**, and White now takes the Knight: **3 Nc3xe4.** Take a look at the next diagram.

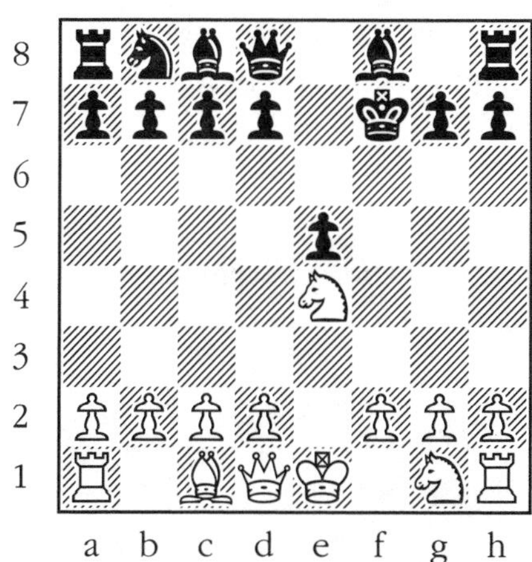

Diagram 9: Black on move

Black's best move now is d7-d5!, grabbing the lion's share of the center. After the Knight retreats, Black can develop his pieces with a good game, and his King can eventually retreat to safety. Instead Black makes an apparently safe, conservative play, only to run into unexpected trouble. He plays **3 ... Nb8-c6?** and White replies with **4 Qd1-f3 check!**

Where should Black put his King? Moving to g6 looks a little too adventurous, while retreating to e8 seems pointless (although that's actually the best play). Instead Black snuggles back to g8, which looks safe enough: **4 ... Kf7-g8**. Black intends to follow with d7-d5 next turn, with a good game.

White however, has other plans. Now he shows Black the shocking point of his play: **5 Ne4-g5!!** White threatens to play Qf3-f7 mate. But wait – isn't the Knight unguarded? Yes, but if Black snaps it off with Qd8xg5, White follows with Qf3-d5 checkmate!

With two checkmates threatened, Black has to figure out a way to guard both f7 and d5 at the same time. That's not so easy. The only move Black can try is Qd8-e7, and after Qf3-d5 check, he can give up his Queen with Qe7-e6. Since that would lose a Queen for a Knight, Black gives up. This example shows the constant danger of an exposed King. None of Black's moves looked silly, but the weakness at f7 led to a quick defeat nonetheless.

Now look at a position where a weakness on f7 shows up in a slightly different way.

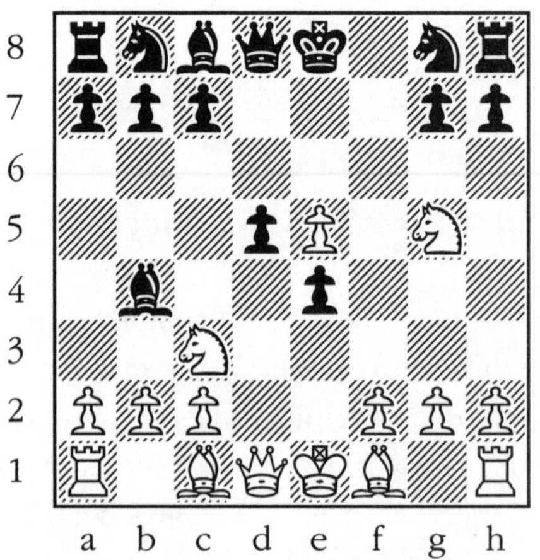

Diagram 10: White on move

Although Black's f-pawn is gone, he seems to have his defenses in order. The Black pawn at d5 effectively blocks the c4-f7 diagonal, preventing White's Bishop from getting into action. The White Queen can give a check by Qd1-h5 check, but Black would block with g7-g6, and the White Queen would have to retreat. White's Knight at g5 looks threatening, but how can he press his attack forward?

White plays **1 e5-e6!** This is the first time we've seen a lowly pawn join in the attack on the f7 square. Now White threatens Ng5-f7, attacking the Queen and trapping the Rook.
Black needs to guard the f7 square again, but first he plays **1 ... Bb4xc3 check**, exchanging off the White Knight. White replies **2 b2xc3.** Now Black defends f7 again with **2 ... Ng8-h6.**

Now White plays **3 Qd1-h5 check!** In the original position, Black could have blocked this check with g7-g6. Now, with the Knight on h6, that's not possible, since White would take the Knight with his Queen. Instead Black has to move his King, **3 ...Ke8-f8.**

White now checks again with **4 Bc1-a3 check!** Black can't interpose without losing his Queen, so his King heads for the corner: **4 ... Kf8-g8.**

Take a look at the next diagram.

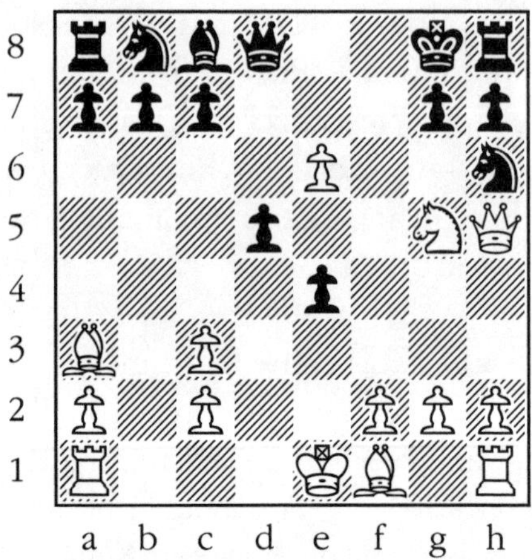

Diagram 11: White on move

Now comes the beautiful finish: White plays **5 Qh5-f7 check!!** Black must play **5 ... Nh6xf7.** And White finishes with **6 e6xf7, checkmate.** White's pawn itself administers the final blow.

Where was Black's decisive error? It was actually the innocuous-looking move Bb4xc3 check. There was no need for Black to capture the Knight, since the Knight was pinned and couldn't move anyway. In addition, the capture opened up the diagonal from c1 to a3, enabling White to bring his dark-squared Bishop into the attack. By forgoing the capture, Black could have preserved his Bishop for defence, while maintaining the option of capturing later anyway.

We'll finish this chapter with an amazing little game illustrating the danger of neglecting the defense of f7. It's a game played at Queen odds, which means White removes his Queen before the game starts. After just six moves, White announces a forced mate in nine more moves, based on an attack against f7!

Watch.

1	**e2-e4**	**e7-e5**
2	**Ng1-f3**	**Nb8-c6**
3	**Bf1-c4**	**Ng8-f6**
4	**Nb1-c3**	**Nc6-a5?**

With an extra Queen, you don't need to do much right to win the game. Simply develop your pieces, contest key squares, and above all exchange pieces whenever possible. The fewer pieces on the board, the less White can do and the more important the advantage of a Queen becomes.

Black's fourth move takes a piece away from the center and loses the e-pawn as well. A better plan was just to develop the King's Bishop, with Bf8-c5 or even Bf8-e7. Still, Black's error is certainly not enough to lose the game.

5	**Nf3xe5**	**Nf6xe4?**

The right idea for Black was to just exchange pieces with Na5xc4, Ne5xc4. Although Black would have lost a pawn, he would have exchanged off White's best attacking piece, the White-squared Bishop.

After Black's move White could take the pawn on f7, but that still wouldn't be decisive. Instead, White sets a clever trap.

6	**d2-d3**	**Ne4-c5??**

Black should have traded pieces with either Na5xc4 (best, eliminating the Bishop) or Ne4xc3 (good enough to win). Instead, he walks into a forced checkmate based on his weak f7 square.

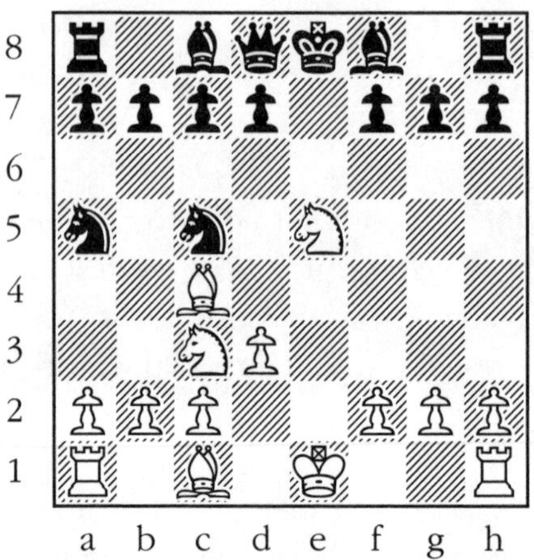

Diagram 12: White on move

White's first job is to draw the Black King out into the open.

7	**Bc4xf7 check**	**Ke8-e7**
8	**Bc1-g5 check**	**Ke7-d6**
9	**Nc3-b5 check!**	

White could have captured Black's Queen, which might have been good enough to win the game, but instead he sees that a checkmate is looming.

9	**...**	**Kd6xe5**
10	**f2-f4 check**	**Ke5-f5**

Black's move is forced, as all his moves have been since White played 7. Bc4xf7. Notice how the White pieces control almost all the squares around the Black King. If White can draw the Black King far enough away from the rest of his army, a checkmate will be possible.

Watch how he does this.

11	**Nb5-d4 check**	**Kf5-g4**
12	**h2-h3 check**	**Kg4-g3**
13	**Nd4-e2 check**	**Kg3xg2**
14	**Bf7-d5 check**	**Nc5-e4**
15	**Bd5xe4 checkmate!**	

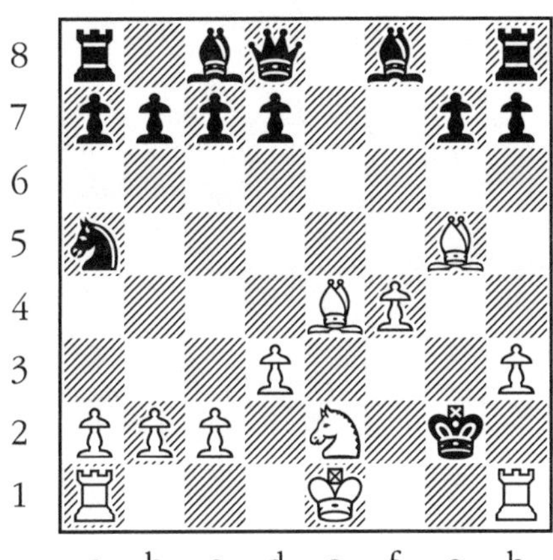

Diagram 13: Black is checkmated.

Amazing! Notice that after Bc4xf7 check, every Black move was forced. The forcing plays made it easy (well, not too difficult anyway) for White to calculate this combination all the way to the end.

5

LEGAL'S MATE

About the year 1750, a powerful attacking idea was discovered by a strong French player, De Kermur, Sire de Legal. Legal was a regular at the Cafe de la Regence in Paris, a combination of bar, restaurant, and night spot where the best players in Paris would congregate. One night in a casual game against Saint Brie, Legal played the following remarkable little game.

	LEGAL	**SAINT BRIE**
1	**e2-e4**	**e7-e5**
2	**Ng1-f3**	**d7-d6**
3	**Bf1-c4**	**Bc8-g4**

Defending the Black e-pawn with d7-d6 on the second move is known as Philidor's defense, named for a pupil of Legal's, Andre Philidor, who was the unofficial World Champion of the last part of the 18th century. It's a perfectly sound, but somewhat cramped defense, which requires accurate play on Black's part.

Playing the Bishop to g4 on the third move isn't a good idea. White will attack the Bishop at some point with h2-h3, and Black will either have to retreat the Bishop, losing time, or exchange the Bishop for White's Knight, accelerating White's development. The move also has some quick tactical drawbacks, as Legal proves in this game.

4	**Nb1-c3**	**g7-g6?**

Although Black's third move was a slight inaccuracy, his fourth move is a full-fledged blunder. (He should have played Nb8-c6.) Now Legal launches his brilliant combination.

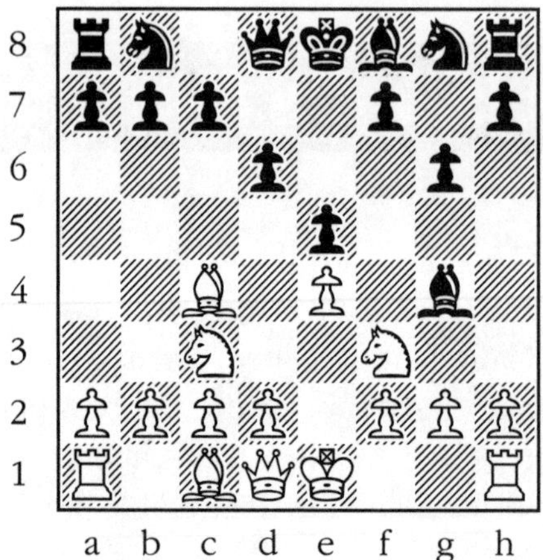

Diagram 14: White (Legal) to move

5	**Nf3xe5!!**	

This move is known as Legal's sacrifice. Ignoring the pin, White sacrifices his Queen to get his Knight to e5. What's his plan?

5	**...**	**Bg4xd1**
6	**Bc4xf7 check**	**Ke8-e7**
7	**Nc3-d5 mate**	

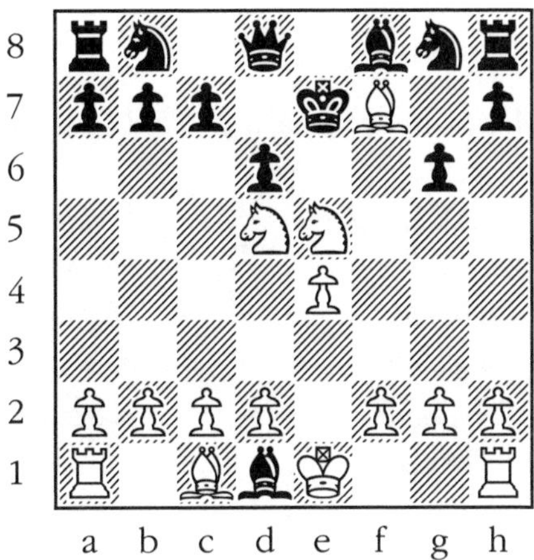

Diagram 15: Final position of Legal's mate

In the final position, White's three minor pieces do yeoman work. The Knight on e5 covers d7 and f7, the Bishop guards e8 and e6, while the Knight on d5 guards f6 while attacking the King on e7. Black is a Queen ahead, but his extra Queen doesn't help him at all.

THE KEY ELEMENTS

The three key elements of Legal's combination are

1. A White Knight on f3, ready to hop to e5.
2. A White Bishop on c4, ready to capture on f7 and flush out the Black King.
3. A Black Bishop on g4, apparently pinning the White Knight but actually vulnerable to attack.

Note that Legal's sacrifice is not really a checkmating combination. In our previous game, if Black could have seen the possible checkmate, he could have escaped defeat by playing d6xe5 on move 5. White would then have played Qd1xg4. White would have lost a Knight but gained a pawn and Bishop in return. A profitable trade to be sure, but the game would have had quite a ways to go.

Now let's look at Legal's combination in a slightly different form.

	TAYLOR	AMATEUR
1	e2-e4	e7-e5
2	Bf1-c4	Ng8-f6
3	Ng1-f3	Nf6xe4
4	Nb1-c3	Ne4xc3
5	d2xc3	

This opening is called the Boden-Kieseritzky Gambit, after the two nineteenth-century players who first studied its complexities. White has sacrificed his e-pawn for an early initiative. (White's Bishop, Knight, and Queen are all active, while Black's pieces are undeveloped.) With good play, Black can hold on and reach an equal game, but there are many traps to snare the unwary player.

5	...	d7-d6
6	0-0	Bc8-g4?

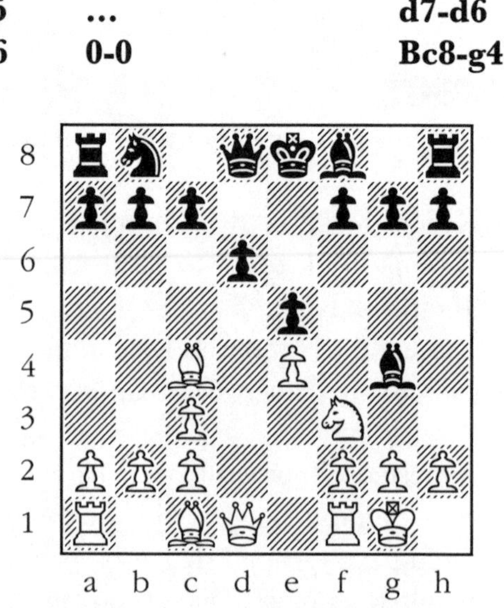

Diagram 16: White on move

As in the previous game, this early Bishop move gets Black into trouble. Bf8-e7 was a better idea.

7	**Nf3xe5!**	**Bg4xd1**
8	**Bc4xf7 check**	**Ke8-e7**
9	**Bc1-g5 checkmate!**	

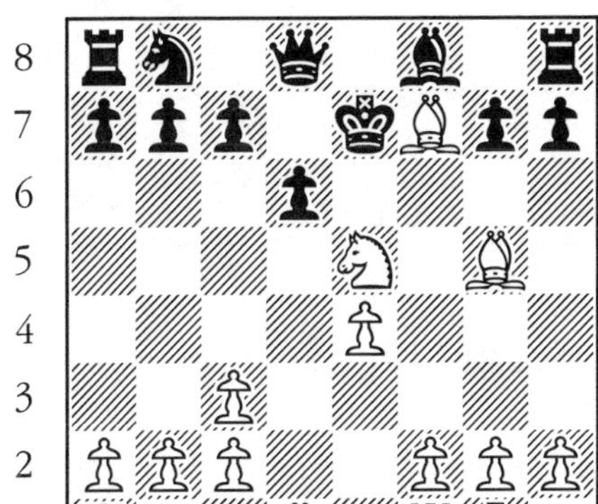

Diagram 17: Black is checkmated

In this game the black-squared Bishop took over the job of the Queen's Knight in our first game. If the e7 square is blocked, the attacking side only needs the c4 Bishop and the e5 Knight to force mate. Take a look at our next game.

	BERGER	**FROLICH**
1	**e2-e4**	**e7-e5**
2	**Nb1-c3**	**Nb8-c6**
3	**Ng1-f3**	**d7-d6**
4	**Bf1-b5**	**Bc8-g4**
5	**Nc3-d5**	**Ng8-e7**
6	**c2-c3**	**a7-a6**
7	**Bb5-a4**	**b7-b5**
8	**Ba4-b3**	**Nc6-a5**

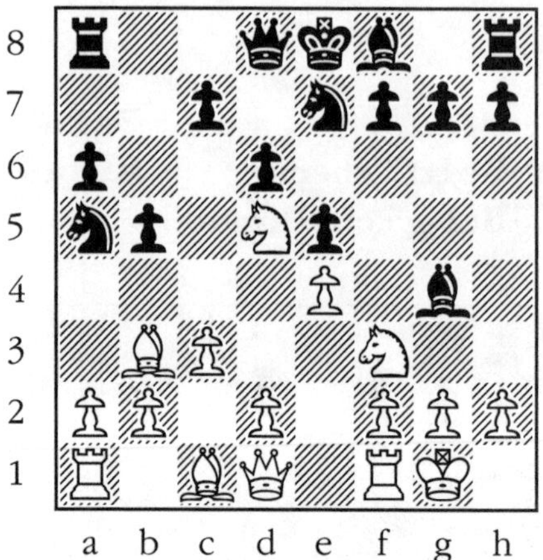

Diagram 18: White on move

Up until his last move, Black had defended reasonably well. On the last turn, he should have tried to untangle his pieces with a move like Ne7-g6. Now White sees the opportunity for a killer combination, based on Legal's sacrifice:

9	**Nf3xe5!!**	

As before, White gives up his Queen to the enemy Bishop. But how can he get his own Bishop to f7?

9	**...**	**Bg4xd1**
10	**Nd5-f6**	**check!**

Here's the idea. The Knight sacrifices itself to clear a path for the Bishop to reach f7. Since it's a check, Black has no choice but to recapture.

10	**...**	**g7xf6**
11	**Bb3xf7 mate**	

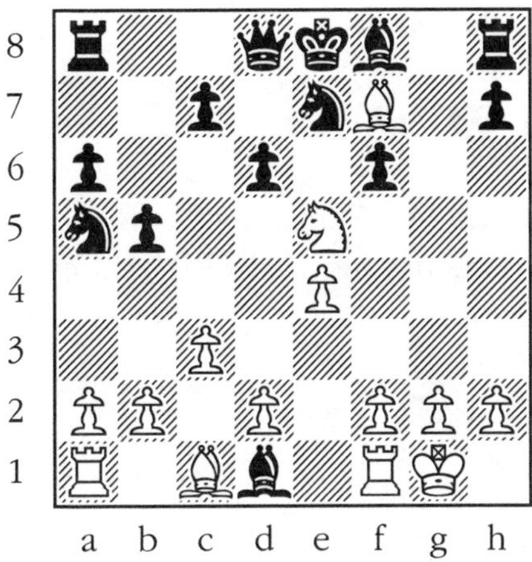

Diagram 19: Black is checkmated

With the Knight at e7 causing Black's pieces to trip over each other, White didn't need as much firepower as in the first two games.

Our last example of Legal's sacrifice comes from a more recent tournament game. White seems to have a good game when he overlooks a possibility of Legal's sacrifice. In this case, the sacrifice is just the first step in an amazing attack that eventually crashes through to victory. Study Black's play in this game carefully; even if the sacrifice doesn't lead to an immediate mate, the long-term attack may be powerful enough for a win.

1	**e2-e4**	**e7-e5**
2	**Ng1-f3**	**Nb8-c6**
3	**Nb1-c3**	**Ng8-f6**

This opening is known, appropriately, as the Four Knight's Game. It's complicated, and requires alert play on both sides.

4	**d2-d4**	**e5xd4**

5	**Nf3xd4**	**Bf8-c5**
6	**Nd4xc6**	**b7xc6**
7	**Bc1-g5**	**d7-d6**
8	**Qd1-e2**	

The first sign of trouble. This blocks the Bishop on f1 from getting into play. A better move was Bf1-d3, preparing to castle on the King's side.

8	**...**	**0-0**
9	**e4-e5?**	

Now White really starts to have problems. If your King is still in the center of the board, you don't want to open up the center files. Instead try to keep the position closed and get your King out of danger. White would have been better off trying moves like f2-f3 or 0-0-0.

9	**...**	**d6xe5**
10	**Nc3-e4**	

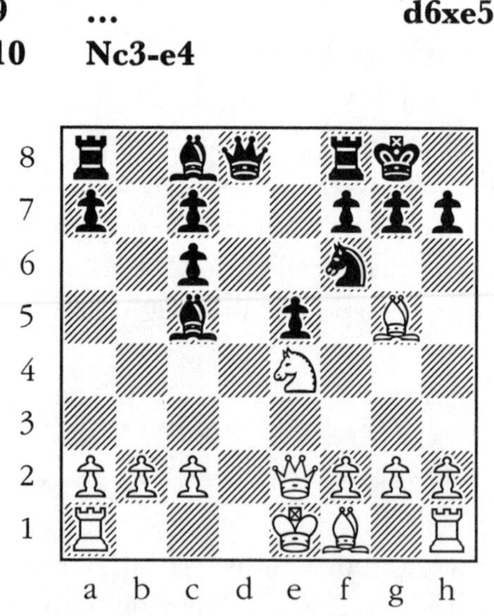

Diagram 20: Black on move

White was aiming for this position with his last move. Since Black's Knight on f6 is pinned, White attacks it again, as well as the loose Black Bishop on c5.

Black could meet all the threats by playing the solid defensive move Bc5-e7, defending everything and remaining a pawn ahead. Instead he sees a brilliant refutation of White's play, starting with Legal's sacrifice:

10	**...**	**Nf6xe4!!**

This must have come as a shock to White! Black ignores the pin and calmly snaps off the Knight. The best is yet to come, however.

11	**Bg5xd8**	**Bc5xf2 check**
12	**Ke1-d1**	

As in most examples of Legal's sacrifice, White could avoid the worst by choosing another line of play. Here, for example, White could capture on f2, giving back the Queen. That would lead to an endgame where White was two pawns down, with grim chances.

White is playing to win, however, since he doesn't yet see how Black can checkmate him. That's actually good strategy on White's part. If you don't see a forced checkmate for your opponent, try to hold onto the sacrificed material. After all, your opponent might have made an unsound sacrifice. Keeping all the sacrificed material may be the easiest way to win.

In this game, however, Black knows what he's doing.

12	**...**	**Rf8xd8 check**
13	**Kd1-c1**	

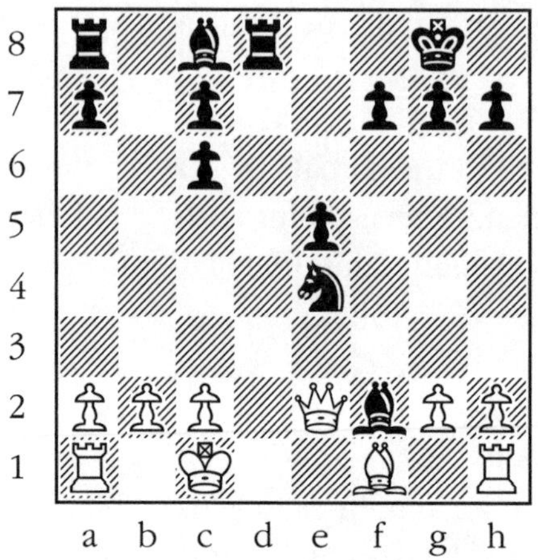

Diagram 21: Black on move

White's King has been pushed around a bit, but he's avoided the checks and now seems relatively safe. The Queen prevents a check by the Black Bishop at e3, and also guards the d2 and d1 squares. So how does Black make progress?

13	**...**	**Bc8-g4!!**

Black finds the answer – what's called a deflection sacrifice.

DEFLECTION

When your opponent has a single piece that's holding his position together, a deflection sacrifice may be the answer. Deflection means giving up a piece to lure the key defender away from the scene of the action. In this case, White's Queen is going to have to leave the key e2 square, where it guards the approaches to White's King.

Note that White can't take the Knight on e4, since Black would play Rd8-d1 checkmate. White has to take the Bishop.

14	**Qe2xg4**	**Bf2-e3 check**
15	**Kc1-b1**	

Now what? Black has pushed the King into the corner, and now he'd like to move his Rook to d1. But the White Queen still guards that square.

15	**...**	**Ne4-d2 check**
16	**Kb1-c1**	**Nd2-f3 discovered check!!**

Black solves his last problem with what's called an interference maneuver. He puts his Knight where it blocks the diagonal from g4 to d1. Now the White Queen can't capture on d1 anymore.

17	**Kc1-b1**	**Rd8-d1 checkmate**

In this game, Legal's sacrifice was just the beginning of a long series of combinational blows. It was a much more difficult game to play than the earlier games in this chapter, because Black had to see the combination through to the end before he sacrificed his Queen on move 10. Remember, if you sacrifice your Queen and you don't actually have a checkmate in mind, you're probably going to lose.

6

THE KING HUNT

The King hunt is a very special, and extremely powerful type of attack. In most attacks, the attacker knows where the enemy King is located, and the main problem is to move enough pieces to the vicinity of the King to deliver checkmate.

King hunts work differently. In a true King hunt, the enemy King is exposed (usually by means of a sacrifice) and then herded out into the open, far away from the defending cover of his own pieces. Exposed and defenseless, he's trapped in a net of enemy pieces and checkmated.

If the enemy King is moved far enough away from the sheltering cover of his own pieces, it may not require much material to deliver a checkmate – simply a couple of pieces might do the trick. For this reason, one of the important techniques of attacking play – the need to calculate the combination through to checkmate – doesn't apply so strongly to King hunts. It's usually enough to see that you can move the King far away from his other pieces.

As long as you have attacking pieces of your own at that point, a checkmating combination or at least a perpetual check is likely.

The difficult part of a King hunt is generally the first few moves of the attack, when the King is exposed and brought out into the open. Since no player will move their King out into battle without very good cause, a surprise sacrifice is usually the method for prying him from his defenses.

Once the King has been exposed, the attacker uses a series of forcing checks to push him farther from home and into enemy territory. In some very rare cases, the King can be pushed away just through a series of threats. We'll show one example of this at the end of this chapter. When the King is completely separated from his army, the final problem is to construct a mating net. The Queen and Rooks are excellent for this purpose, although sometimes the Bishops and Knights will suffice to do the job.

Our first game is from the mid-nineteenth century, between the German star Max Lange (White) and von Schierstedt.

MAX LANGE		VON SCHIERSTEDT
1	**e2-e4**	**e7-e5**
2	**Ng1-f3**	**Nb8-c6**
3	**d2-d4**	**e5xd4**
4	**Bf1-b5**	**Bf8-c5**
5	**0-0**	**Ng8-e7**

The opening in this game is actually a hybrid of two openings, the Ruy Lopez and the Scotch Game. Both sides are developing well and no one has a significant advantage yet.

6	**Nb1-d2**	**d7-d5**
7	**e4xd5**	**Qd8xd5**
8	**Bb5-c4**	**Qd5-d8**
9	**Nf3-g5**	**Nc6-e5**

Black would like to castle and get his King out of the center, but White's last move prevented castling. If Black had played 9 ... 0-0, White would have replied 10 Qd1-h5, threatening 11 Qh5xh7 checkmate. If Black then played 10 ... Bc8-f5, stopping the mate by protecting h7, White would play Ng5xf7! with a winning advantage.

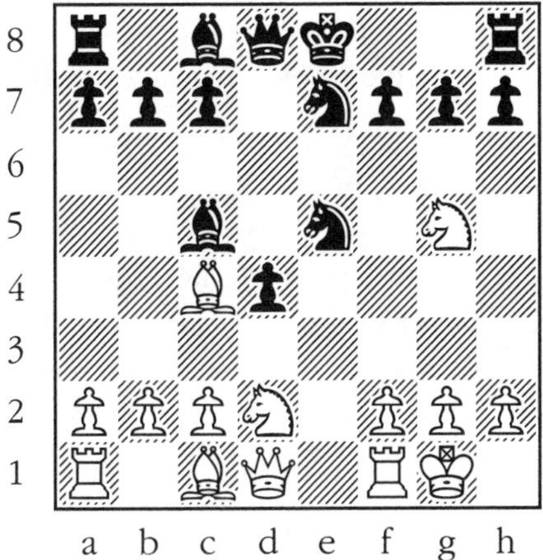

Diagram 22: White to move

10	**Ng5xf7!**	**Ne5xf7**
11	**Bc4xf7 check**	**Ke8xf7**
12	**Qd1-h5 check!**	**g7-g6**
13	**Qh5xc5**	

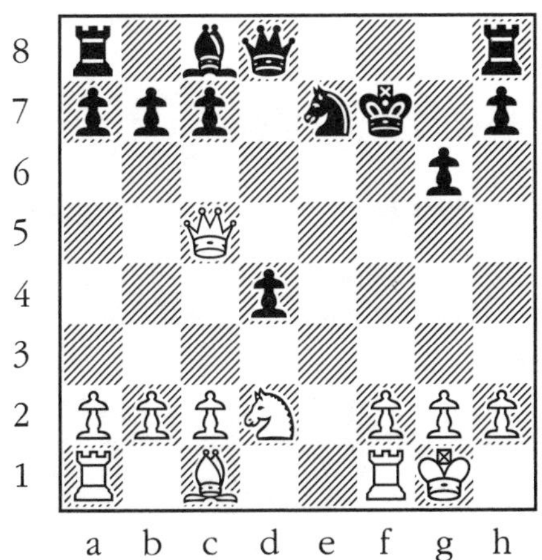

Diagram 23: Black to move

LOSING THE CASTLING OPTION

White's combination on the last four moves was really just an extended exchange. Both sides lost a Knight and a Bishop, while White regained the pawn he had sacrificed on move 3. The important feature of the exchange, however, was that the Black King lost the right to castle.

Losing the right to castle isn't necessarily fatal. If Black has enough time, he can easily repair the damage. By playing moves like Kf7-g7, Rh8-e8, and Bc8-f5, he could construct a perfectly secure position for his King.

The key question is: Will he have the time? If White plays carelessly, with routine developing moves, Black will accomplish his goal. If White can operate with threats, however, Black may not have the time. He may not be able to meet White's threats and secure his King all at once.

In Diagram 23, White already has a threat: to win Black's d-pawn by attacking it with Nd2-f3 and Rf1-d1. Black can meet the threat, but not in a way that secures his King.

13 ... Ne7-c6

Protects the pawn with the Knight.

14 Nd2-f3 Rh8-e8

Black develops his Rook, thinking he will soon be able to move his King back to safety.

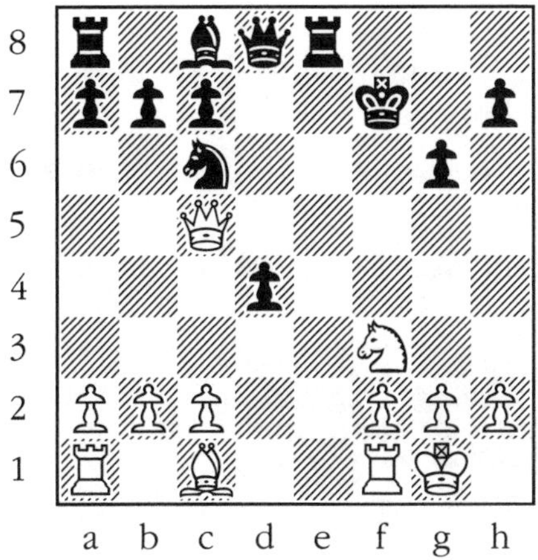

Diagram 24: White to move

15	**Bc1-h6!**	

A nice move, more difficult to find than many sacrifices. White denies Black the use of the g7 square as a retreat for the King.

15	**...**	**Bc8-f5**
16	**Ra1-e1**	**Qd8-d7**
17	**Qc5-c4 check**	**Bf5-e6**
18	**Nf3-g5 check**	**Kf7-f6**

The King can't retreat to g8 without losing the Bishop on e6. The King instead goes to f6, where it keeps the Bishop triply defended. If White exchanges on e6, he will just reach an equal ending.

Notice, however, that the Black King's retreat route has now been completely cut off. The White Bishop controls g7 and f8, and the Knight controls f7. If White can figure out a way to get at the King, Black could be in severe danger. However, that doesn't seem to be so easy. Meanwhile, White must move his Queen.

19 Qc4-e2!

Threatening Qe2-f3, and meanwhile setting a subtle trap.

19 ... Be6-g4

This protects f3 and attacks the White Queen as well.

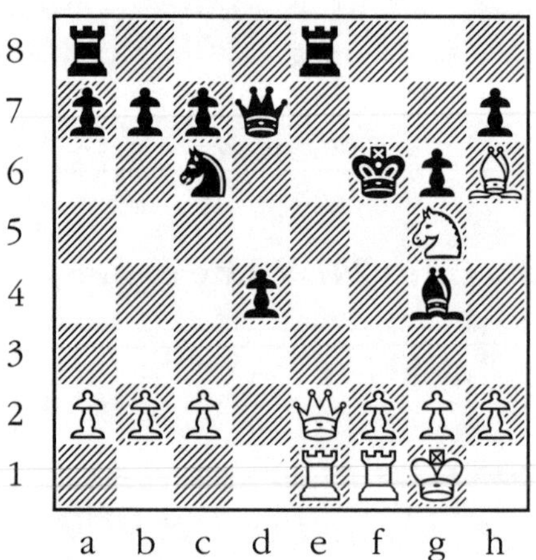

Diagram 25: White on move

Black's King is vulnerable but White needs a way to get at him. The problem is that White's Rooks are bottled up, one blocked by the Queen and one by White's own f-pawn. How can White open up the position so his pieces can get loose?

20 f2-f3!!

When Black takes the Queen, White will finally get the open lines he needs.

20 ... Re8xe2
21 f3xg4 discovered check

As a result of the sacrifice, all four of White's remaining pieces are fully activated against Black's King. White's next job is to get the King as far away from Black's defensive pieces (the Queen and the Knight) as possible. Let's see how White manages this.

21 ... Kf6-e5

The first point of White's brilliant sacrifice is that Black cannot escape to the safety of the first rank. If Black tries 21 ... Kf6-e7 22 Re1xe2 check Ke7-d8, White wins with Rf1-f8 check. In order to avoid this checkmating pattern, Black has to move his King over to the d-file and then the c-file.

22 Re1xe2 check Ke5-d5

This move is forced to avoid losing the Queen. If Black plays 22 ... Ke5-d6, White gets the Black Queen with a Knight fork: 23 Ng5-e4 check Kd6-d5 24 Ne4-f6 check! Now, however, White seems a bit stymied. He has no effective checks and the Black King threatens to escape to b6 via c5.

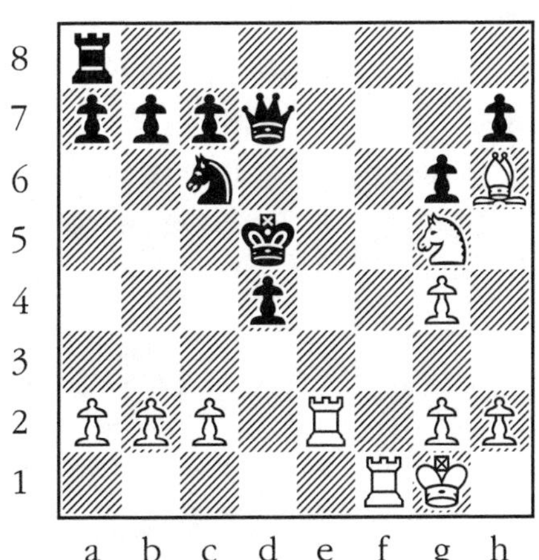

Diagram 26: White on move

23 Ng5-e4!

THE POWER OF QUIET MOVES

These quiet moves in the middle of an attack are the most difficult to foresee (for either side). White is continuing the attack by means of a bunch of threats against Black's Queen. White's immediate threat is to win the Queen by Ne4-f6 check. If Black tries to move the King back with 23 ... Kd5-e6, White wins the Queen with Ne4-c5 check. Notice that if White is able to win the Queen for his Knight, he'll be a Rook ahead with an easily winning game.

Black must find a way to keep his Queen safe, but with the White Rooks sweeping the e-file and f-file, that's not so easy.

23 ... Kd5-c4

Black leaves the Queen where it is and instead steps out to c4, avoiding all the Knight forks. Unfortunately the King is getting farther and farther away from home.

24 a2-a4!

Another fine non-checking move, difficult to see in advance. The point of this move is to cut off the square b5 from the Black King. With c5 controlled by the White Knight and d5 unavailable because of the fork at f6, the King has been cut off from his own side of the board.

24 ... Qd7xg4

This move doesn't just win a pawn, it also stirs up some trouble because of the attack on the Rook at e2.

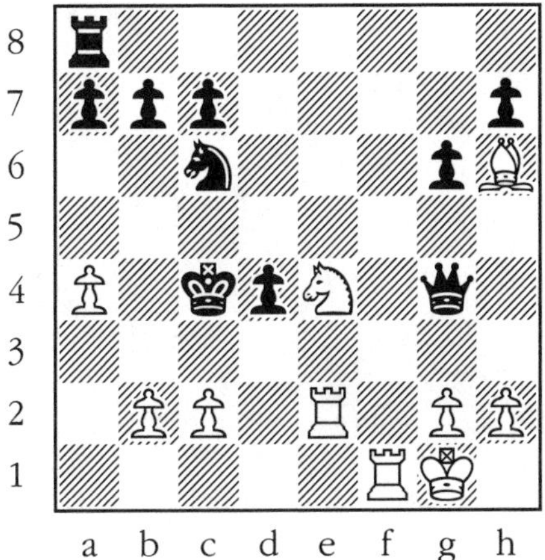

Diagram 27: White on move

Now White plays a couple of forcing checks to drive the Black King even farther away from his supporting cast.

25 b2-b3 check Kc4-b4

The King can't retreat to d5 because White still has the fork Ne4-f6 check, winning the Black Queen. Now however, the King threatens to get away via a5 and a6.

26 Bh6-d2 check!

The Bishop has done its job at h6 and now gets back into the action. With only a few pieces left, everyone must do his part. The Bishop checks the King at b4 and also controls the a5 square, driving the Black King into the corner.

26 ... Kb4-a3

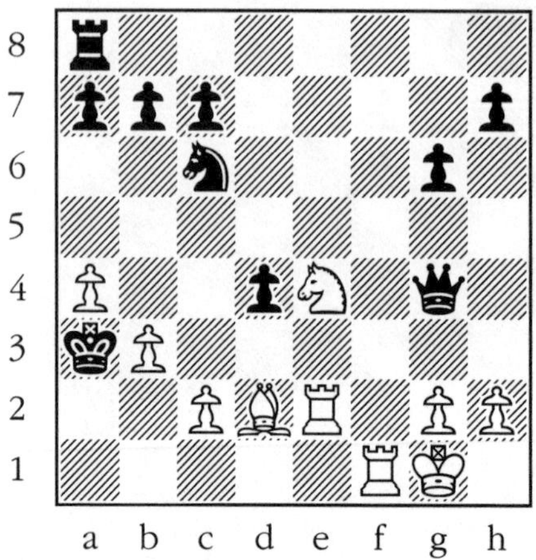

Diagram 28: White on move

White has now succeeded in his job of separating the Black King from his army. The King is confined to the squares a3, a2, and b2, and Black's Queen and Rook are far away. At this point White needs to find an actual checkmating combination.

Remember that time is on Black's side. Given a few free moves, Black could mobilize his Rook and Knight and break the back of White's attack. White's pieces are fully developed, so the time for him to strike is now. But what's the key move?

27 Ne4-c3!!

This is it. White threatens checkmate in two moves: 28 Rf1-a1 check, and then either ... Ka3-b2 29 Ra1-a2 checkmate or ... Ka3-b4 29 Nc3-e4 discovered checkmate!

27	**...**	**d4xc3**
28	**Bd2xc3**	

Now there's a new threat: Rf1-a1 checkmate. The Rook on e2 has been left undefended, but Black doesn't have time to take it. The only way to stop this mate is to bring the Knight up to block on a2.

28	**...**	**Nc6-b4**
29	**Rf1-a1 check**	**Nb4-a2**

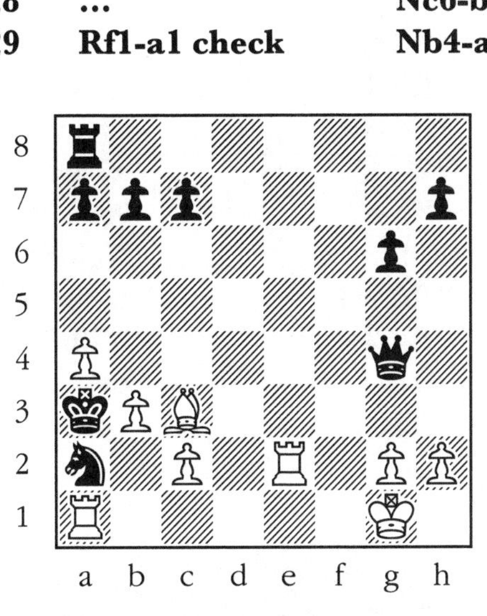

Diagram 29: White on move

Has Black finally found a defense? It would seem that White is running out of pieces.

30	**Ra1xa2 check!**	**Ka3xa2**
31	**Re2-e1!**	

The final coup. Black now cannot prevent checkmate by Re1-a1. A tremendous game.

This battle illustrated many of the ideas of the basic King hunt. At every stage of the game White anticipated Black's attempts to get his King back to the relative safety of his own lines, and was able to thwart them either by directly controlling the escape squares, or by using the threats of Knight forks winning the Black Queen. At the end, the Black King was so isolated that White was able to effect checkmate with just his last two pieces. Our next game is from a more recent tournament, the Chess Olympiad at Lugano, Switzerland in 1968.

	PRINS	**DAY**
1	**e2-e4**	**c7-c5**
2	**Ng1-f3**	**e7-e6**
3	**c2-c4**	**a7-a6**
4	**Bf1-e2**	**Nb8-c6**
5	**0-0**	**Ng8-f6**
6	**Nb1-c3**	**Qd8-c7**
7	**a2-a3**	**b7-b6**
8	**d2-d4**	**c5xd4**
9	**Nf3xd4**	

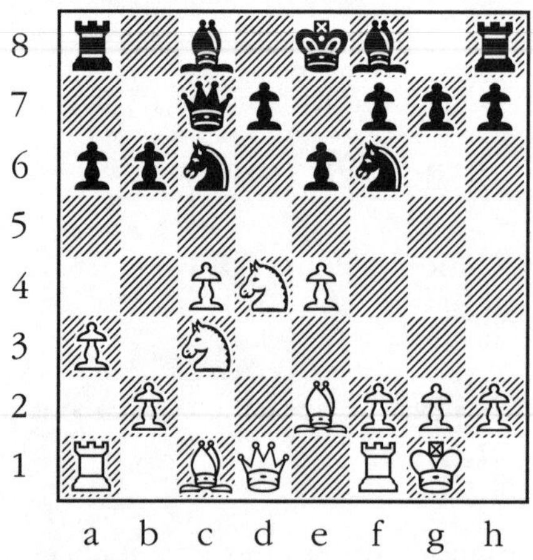

Diagram 30: Black on move

The opening starting with c7-c5 for Black is known as the Sicilian Defense. It usually leads to an unbalanced game, with White attacking on the King-side and Black on the Queen-side. It's an excellent choice for players who like to fight for the initiative from the first move, and it's the most popular defense to e2-e4 in modern tournaments.

Although Black's natural area of expansion is on the Queen-side, that's not his only possibility. The opening is flexible enough so that, under the right circumstances, Black can move on the King-side as well.

9	**...**	**Bc8-b7**
10	**Bc1-e3**	**Bf8-d6**

This development is a little unusual for Black, but not bad. The common development for Black is Bf8-e7 and d7-d6, with a solid defensive structure.

Black's move to d6 starts an attack on the pawn at h2, and indicates that Black may be planning a King-side attack. Right now Black simply threatens Bd6xh2 check.

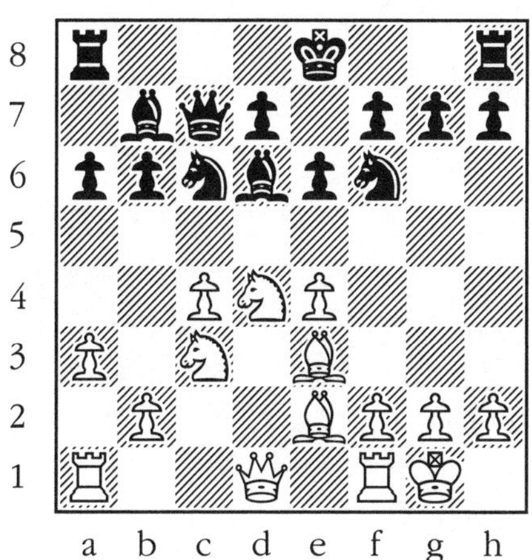

Diagram 31: White to move

11 h2-h3?

Black's aggressive development pays off as White makes a very conservative response. A much better response was to seize some ground in the center with f2-f4, with a counter-threat of e4-e5, winning a piece with a pawn fork. Black would have to meet this threat (probably by playing Nc6xd4 and e7-e5), and a complex game would ensue.

11	**...**	**Bd6-e5**
12	**Qd1-d3**	**h7-h5**

Very bold. Black is planning a King-side attack and he's not shy about advertising his plans. The obvious question at this point is: "Why can't White drive Black back with 13 f2-f4?" In fact, Black has prepared a subtle trap against this obvious move. After 13 f2-f4, Black would play Nc6xd4!

If White then played 14 Be3xd4, Black would play Be5xf4, winning a pawn. If instead White played 14 f4xe5, Black would play Nd4xe2 check, 15 Qd3xe2 Qc7xe5, also winning a pawn.

Instead White ignores Black's maneuvers and prepares to advance on the Queen-side.

13	**Rf1-c1**	**Be5-h2 check**

This check isn't really dangerous, since Black can't get any more pieces to the attack. But it continues the process of loosening the defenses around White's King.

14	**Kg1-f1**	**Nc6-e5**

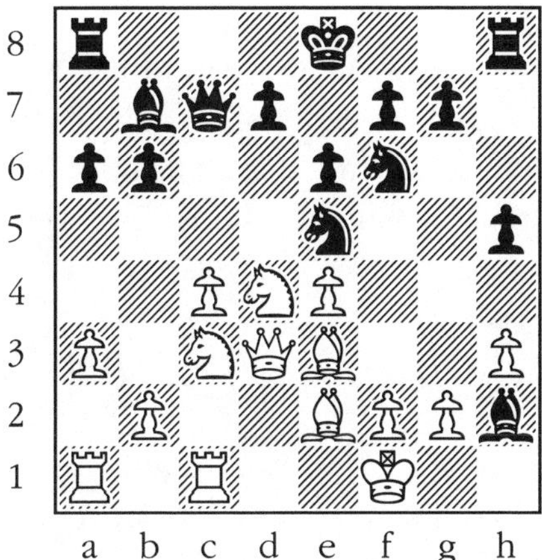

Diagram 32: White to move

With Black's last move, he attacks the Queen at d3 as well as the pawn at c4. In addition, he uncovers an attack against the pawn at e4 by the Bishop back at b7. Can White find a way to save both pawns?

What follows over the next few moves is a series of thrusts and counterthrusts. Black wants to win either the e4 or the c4-pawn, or both. White has worked out an ingenious line of defense, based on surrendering the e4-pawn in return for eventually winning the Black pawn at b6.

It might appear during this line of play that the idea of a Black attack against the White King has been forgotten. Actually White has forgotten about it, but Black is still thinking of the attack as a long-range possibility. But for the time being, the skirmishing is over the squares e4, c4, and b6.

15	**Qd3-d1**	**Nf6xe4**
16	**Nc3-a4**	**Ne4-c5**
17	**Na4xb6!?**	**Qc7xb6**

18 Nd4-f3

This move is the point of White's temporary Knight sacrifice. He is attacking the undefended Bishop at h2 as well as pinning the Black Knight at c5. White threatens both Nf3xh2 and b2-b4, winning the pinned Knight. Thus, he is certain to regain his piece.

18 ... Qb6-c6!

This saves the Bishop on h2 by means of another pin – the White Knight on f3 is pinned against his own pawn on g2. If White plays Nf3xh2, Black replies Qc6xg2 check, winning.

19 Be3xc5

If Black captures on c5, White will then be free to take the Bishop on h2.

19 ... Bh2-f4!

Now Black attacks both the Bishop on c5 and the Rook on c1.

20 Bc5-e3 Bf4xe3
21 f2xe3

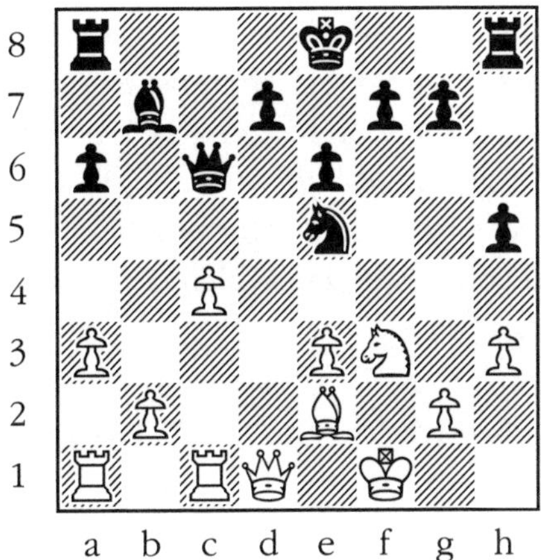

Diagram 33: Black on move

The smoke has cleared from the battle over the White pawns on e4 and c4. White has managed to maintain material equality, and his pawn at c4 is now well-defended. Black's play has extracted some concessions, however. The White King-side now looks a little loose, with the squares h2 and g3 unguarded, the f-file open, and a weak, undefended pawn at e3. With sufficient time, White could repair these weaknesses with defensive moves like Qd1-d4, Rc1-c3, and Ra1-d1. If Black wants to launch an attack against the White King, the time will have to be now.

21 ... Ne5-g4!!

Black finds a way to expose the White King even more, at the cost of a Knight.

The Knight threatens Ng4xe3 check, forking the King and Queen. If White captures the Knight, Black will recapture with the h-pawn, opening the h-file for the Black Rook at h8 to move down the board.

DON'T BE BLUFFED

White sees that Black will have a dangerous attack, but he doesn't see any forced win. Under the circumstances, his response is reasonable. He takes the Knight and says "Show me." In chess, you can't let your opponent bluff you. If he offers a piece and you can't see a forced loss after capturing, then by all means take the piece. Not all your opponents will have an idea as ingenious as Black's in this game.

22	**h3xg4**	**h5xg4**

Since Black has the possibility of Qc6xg2 check after the Knight moves, White must be careful about where he places the Knight. The only square the Knight can move where it also guards g2 is e1.

23	**Nf3-e1**	**Rh8-h1 check**
24	**Kf1-f2**	

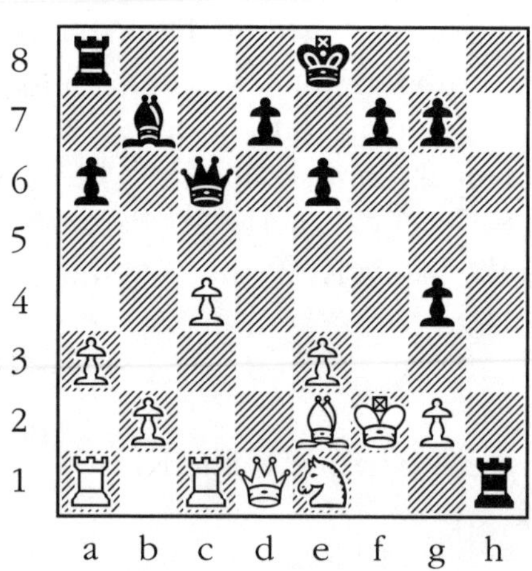

Diagram 34: Black to move

The King hunt process that we saw in the last game has begun. This time the Black Rook has cut off the White King from the comparative safety of his first rank. Now Black has to answer the question, "How can the White King be forced further out?"

One obvious idea suggests itself. Black would like to be able to play Qc6xg2 check, but the g2-pawn is guarded by the Knight on e1. Black, however, is now in position to capture the Knight on e1, removing the guard. Should he play Rh1xe1?

The answer is no. Although this move would work wonderfully if White replied with Qd1xe1?? allowing Qc6xg2 checkmate, White could simply play Kf2xe1. Then after Black captured on g2, White would play Ke1-d2, and his King would be quite safe.

Moving the enemy King around the board isn't an end in itself. If the King can reach a defensible fortress, even on the other side of the board, you haven't necessarily gained anything. It's only if you can haul the King away from the defending pieces that a King hunt can work.

So how can Black expose the White King further?

24 ... g4-g3 check!

This is the key move, which White probably overlooked when he captured Black's Knight on move 22. By moving the White King to g3 before capturing the pawn on g2, Black ensures that the King will be pushed all the way out to the fourth rank, far away from his other pieces.

25 Kf2xg3

Forced.

25 ... Rh1xe1!

Now this idea works.

26	**Qd1xe1**	

No real choice here. If White tries a counterattack by 26 Be2-f3, Black plays Qc6-c7 check and then captures the White Queen next turn.

26	**...**	**Qc6xg2 check**
27	**Kg3-f4**	

If White tries 27 Kg3-h4, Black can play 0-0-0, threatening Rd8-h8 checkmate.

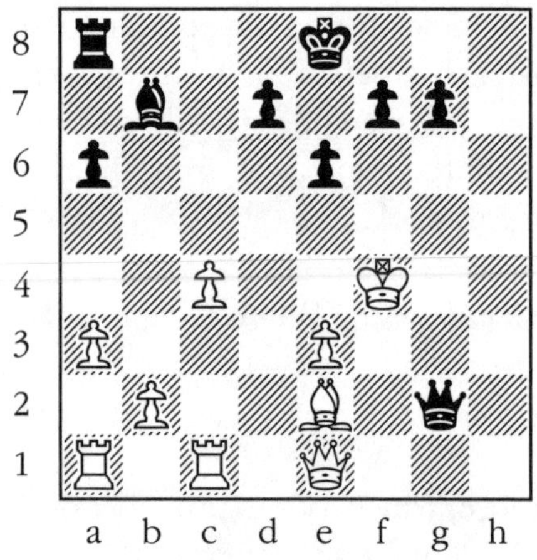

Diagram 35: Black on move

27	**...**	**g7-g5 check**

In a King hunt, even the pawns have to do their part!

28	**Kf4-e5**	**Qg2-e4 check**

At this point White gave up, as he saw that the following mating sequence could not be avoided:

29	Ke5-f6	Qe4-f5 check
30	Kf6-g7	Qf5-g6 check
31	Kg7-h8	0-0-0 checkmate!

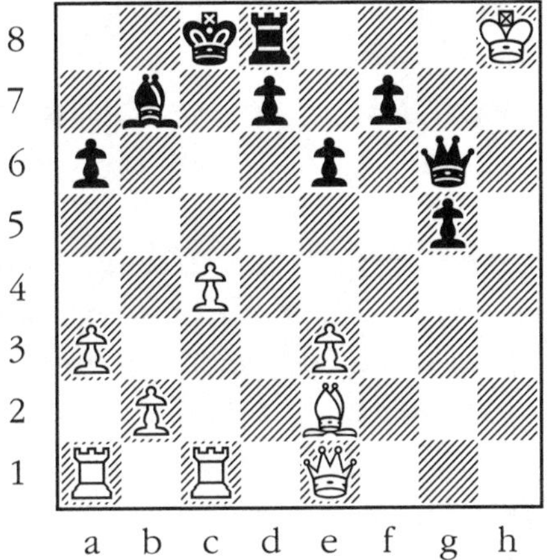

Diagram 36: Final position

Checkmate by castling – rare indeed.

Notice in this last game how much easier Black's task was than in the previous game, once he had pushed the enemy King out into the open. With just a few forced checks, he was able to push the White King up to h8, where there was a simple checkmate. The first game, by contrast, required tremendous ingenuity on White's part to herd the King into a corner and find a checkmate.

The difference was the presence of the Black Queen in the second game. The Queen is such a powerful piece that she can move the enemy King where she wants him to go almost by herself. Since Black didn't have to sacrifice the Queen to expose the White King, his later job was much easier.

We can boil this into a simple rule: If you have to sacrifice your Queen to start a King hunt, you must calculate the continuation more accurately. It's easier for the King to escape the mating net if he doesn't have a Queen to worry about.

Our next King hunt is going to start with the maneuver we learned in the last chapter – Legal's sacrifice.

	VUCINIC	**DJUROVIC**
1	**e2-e4**	**Ng8-f6**

An unusual but sound opening known as Alekhine's Defense. Black immediately counterattacks the e-pawn with his Knight. The strategic idea of Alekhine's Defense is an interesting one: Black is going to use his Knight as a decoy to induce White's center pawns to advance. Later, Black will attack the White center from the sides, hoping it will prove overextended. It's an exciting opening, leading to very sharp, double-edged play.

In 1972, Bobby Fischer surprised Boris Spassky with this opening and defeated him in the critical 13th game of their famous match.

2 Nb1-c3

Conservative play. The main line is 2 e4-e5, followed by d2-d4 and c2-c4. White may be indicating he's uncomfortable with the opening.

2	**...**	**d7-d5**
3	**e4xd5**	**Nf6xd5**
4	**Bf1-c4**	**Nd5-b6**
5	**Bc4-b3**	**Nb8-c6**

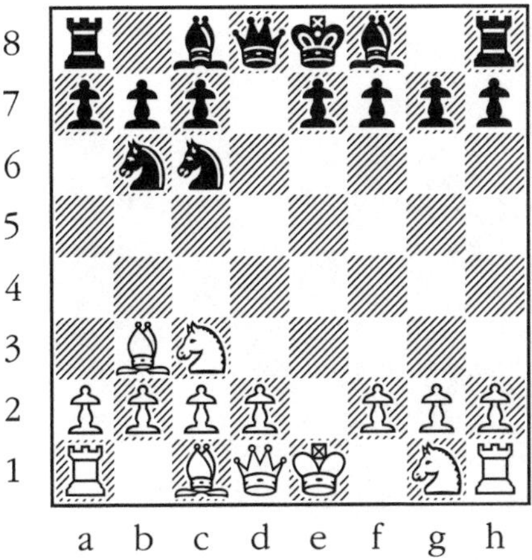

Diagram 37: White on move

An unusual position. White, respecting the counterattacking possibilities of Alekhine's Defense, has declined to build any pawn center at all! Black, as a result, has nothing to attack. Since both sides have developed two minor pieces, the game is about even.

6	**Ng1-f3**	**e7-e5**

Now it's Black who grabs a share of the center!

7	**d2-d3**	**Bc8-g4**

As we've seen in previous games, this early development of the Bishop can get Black into trouble unless he follows up properly. A slightly safer way of developing was Bf8-e7 followed by 0-0.

8	**h2-h3**	**Bg4-h5?**

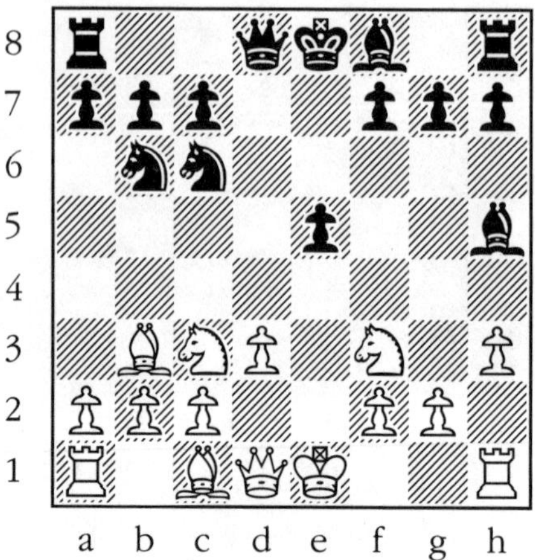

Diagram 38: White on move

If you remember what we learned in the last chapter, White now has a chance to make Legal's sacrifice. He can capture the Black pawn on e5, sacrificing his Queen. The question he has to answer is this: Is the sacrifice sound?

If he decides the sacrifice isn't sound, or doesn't offer wonderful attacking chances, he won't make it, of course. In that case he can proceed quietly, with normal developing moves like Bc1-e3, 0-0, or even g2-g4, chasing away the Bishop.

The first question to ask about a sacrifice is simply "What happens if my opponent doesn't accept it?" If your opponent can decline your sacrifice with a good game, then the sacrifice is really a gamble. Here that's not a problem. If, after 9 Nf3xe5, Black declines the Queen sacrifice and just takes the Knight with 9 ... Nc6xe5, White can play 10 Qd1xh5, capturing the Bishop with a solid extra pawn. So to refute the sacrifice, Black must accept it.

Next question: Does the sacrifice lead to a forced checkmate? In our earlier examples with Legal's sacrifice, it usually led to a quick mate. Here White sees that's not going to be the case, because the square d6 is not occupied by a Black pawn. After the sequence 9 Nf3xe5 Bh5xd1 10 Bb3xf7 check Ke8-e7, the move 11 Bc1-g5 check isn't mate, because Black has the escape square d6 open to his King.

BUILDING A WALL

Looking a little farther into the position, however, White sees a way to construct a wall behind the Black King – an impassible barrier of squares through which the King won't be able to retreat. The possibility of building a wall convinces White that the sacrifice is probably sound and likely to yield a winning attack. So off we go!

9 Nf3xe5!! Bh5xd1

Black accepts the sacrifice. Declining it leads to just a bad game, one pawn down. If the attack doesn't work, Black will win with his extra material.

10 Bb3xf7 check Ke8-e7

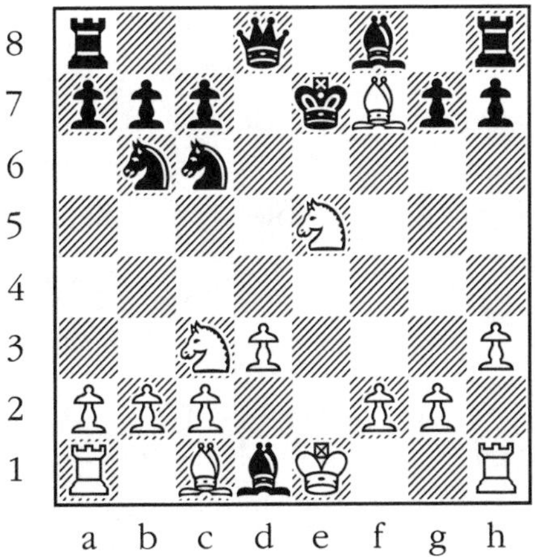

Diagram 39: White on move

In some of our previous Legal's sacrifice examples, White had the possibility of Nc3-d5 check here. But the position of the Black Knight on b6, guarding d5, rules that out here. White's only continuation is with the Bishop check. If the d6 square weren't available to Black's King, the check on g5 would be mate.

11 Bc1-g5 check Ke7-d6

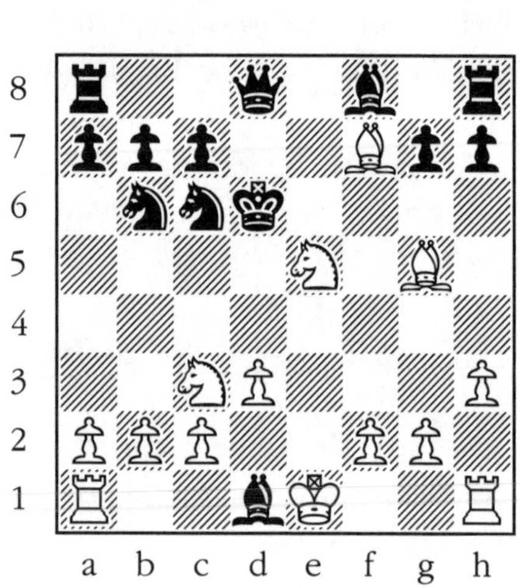

Diagram 40: White on move

Now what? The Black King has reached d6 and now threatens to escape via c5 or pick off the Knight on e5. The Black Bishop on d1 can take the pawn on c2, avoiding capture at the same time. The Queen on d8 is threatening the Bishop on g5. Meanwhile, Black is a full Queen ahead. White, however, is on move. He'd better make good use of that move.

The obvious possibility is 12 Bg5xd8. That at least wins back the Queen. However, it won't win the game. Black would reply 12 ... Nc6xd8, attacking both the Knight at e5 and the Bishop at f7. One of those pieces would have to go, and Black would emerge with a solid extra piece, enough to win the game.

Instead, White finds a brilliant way to continue the attack, by building a wall behind the Black King.

12 Nc3-e4 check! Kd6xe5

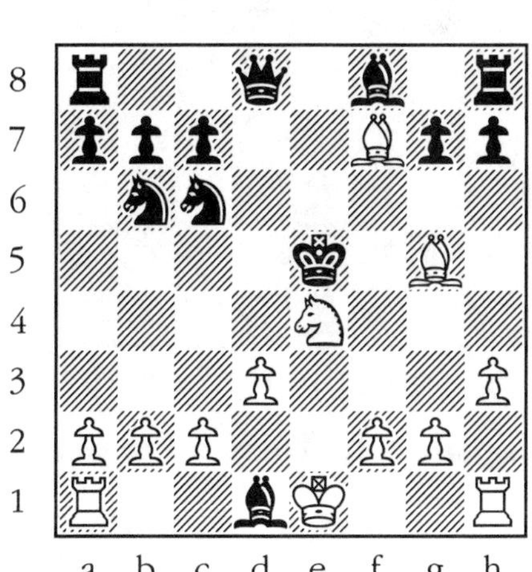

Diagram 41: White on move

By moving to e4, the Knight simultaneously guarded c5, preventing the Black King from escaping to the Queenside. Of course, White had to concede the loss of the Knight on e5.

Now, however, the combination of the Knight on e4 and the Bishop on f7 has constructed a solid wall of control behind the Black King. Take a look at the next diagram, where the squares controlled by the Knight and Bishop are marked with the '+' symbol:

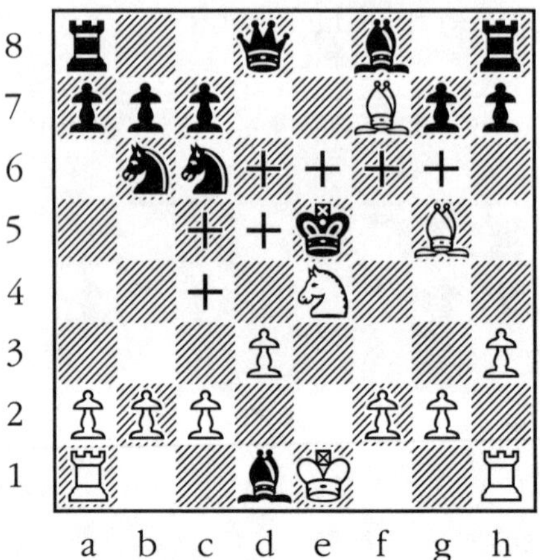

Diagram 42: The wall in place

From c4 over to g6, Black's retreat route is completely cut off. The Black King is now confined to the lower right-hand corner of the board. White's job is now to find a way to checkmate him somewhere in that area.

COORDINATING KNIGHT AND BISHOP

Incidentally, here's a strategic point: When a Knight and Bishop are located on squares of the same color, they control squares of opposite color. This arrangement lets the two pieces work together with maximum efficiency, as Diagram 42 shows. A good tip to remember.

Now let's watch White continue the attack.

13 f2-f4 check Ke5-d4

Black had no choice here. If he tried to escape to the other side, with Ke5-f5, White had Ne4-g3 checkmate.

14 Ra1xd1!

An easy mistake for White to make was 14 Ke1-d2, which threatens c2-c3 mate. This looks strong, but Black could just play Bd1xc2!, eliminating the pawn and leaving White no easy way to make progress. Black's King would still be stuck in the center, but White would have a shortage of pieces to deliver check.

Remember, if you've already sacrificed your Queen, the King hunt must be very precise. There's not much margin for error.

14 ... Qd8xg5

Black is willing to give back some material to break the force of the attack.

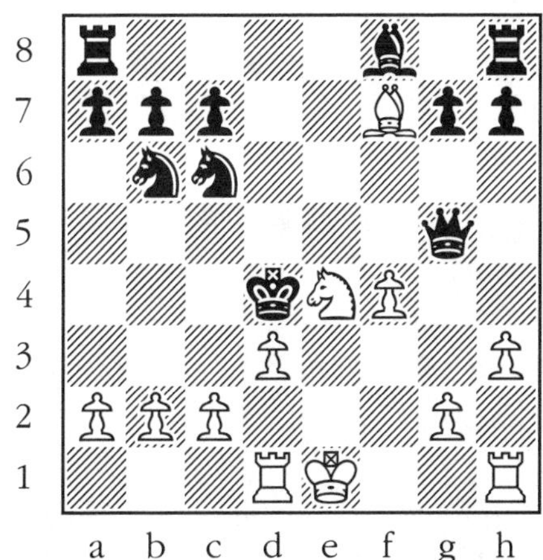

Diagram 43: White to move

15 c2-c3 check! Kd4-e3
16 0-0!

This nice move quietly boxes in the enemy King. If Black tries 16 ... Qg5xf4, White has 17 Rf1-e1 checkmate.

16 ... Qg5-h4

This lets White execute his main threat.

17	**Rf1-f3 check**	**Ke3-e2**
18	**Rd1-d2 check**	**Ke2-e1**
19	**Rf3-f1 mate!**	

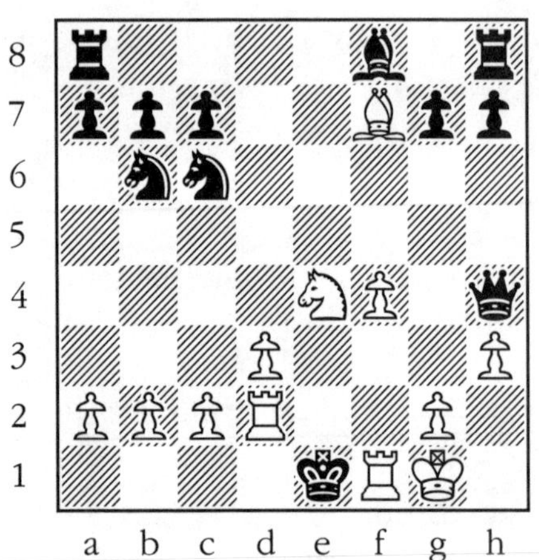

Diagram 44: The final position

As before, without a Queen to assist in the attack, White's King hunt was a very close affair. One careless move at any point and Black could have escaped.

Our last game of this chapter is unique in several ways. The eventual winner is Mikhail Botvinnik, World Champion from 1948 to 1963 (with a couple of brief interruptions). The loser, Svetozar Gligorich, was considered one of the world's top-20 players during the 1950s and 1960s. And the actual King hunt itself, once begun, involves no checks whatever!

A remarkable game.

BOTVINNIK		GLIGORICH
1	c2-c4	g7-g6
2	g2-g3	c7-c5
3	Bf1-g2	Bf8-g7
4	Nb1-c3	Nb8-c6
5	Ng1-f3	Ng8-h6

The game begins with what is called the English Opening, a fairly non-committal line of play. White moves his c-pawn and fianchettos his King's Bishop. Black is under little pressure and, in the absence of direct threats, has the freedom to develop his pieces as he chooses. Botvinnik was justly famous for his deep understanding of these systems.

In this game, Black chooses to simply copy White's moves for awhile. With his fifth move, Black breaks the symmetry, trying to move his Knight to an active post at f5. Botvinnik counters by starting immediate action on the King-side.

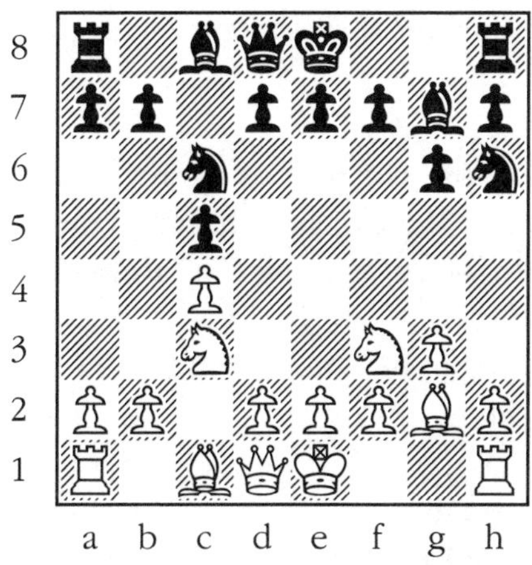

Diagram 45: White on move

6 h2-h4!

White expands on the King-side, preparing to gain more space with h4-h5. Since White hasn't castled on the King-side, he doesn't have to be as careful about moving the King-side pawns as he would normally be. His King can still castle on the Queen-side, or he may decide to just leave the King in the center, where the pawns are undisturbed.

6	**...**	**d7-d6**
7	**d2-d3**	**Ra8-b8**

These slow positional openings are characteristic of a lot of modern tournament play. The players are like boxers bobbing and weaving, waiting for a clear weakness before throwing a punch.

Black's last move might look mysterious but actually has two ideas behind it. First, Black wants to remove his Rook from the h1-a8 diagonal, so that it won't become exposed to an attack by the White Bishop on g2 at some future point. Second, Black wants to launch an attack on the Queen side by playing b7-b5, and he'll prepare for this thrust by playing moves like Ra8-b8, a7-a6, and Bc8-d7.

If this seems like a slow plan to you, you're right. It is. However, in an opening where the two sides haven't really come to grips with each other yet, such slow maneuvers are perfectly acceptable.

Now the game starts to heat up as White continues with his attack down the h-file.

8	**h4-h5**	**Bc8-d7**
9	**Bc1xh6**	**Bg7xh6**
10	**h5xg6**	**h7xg6**

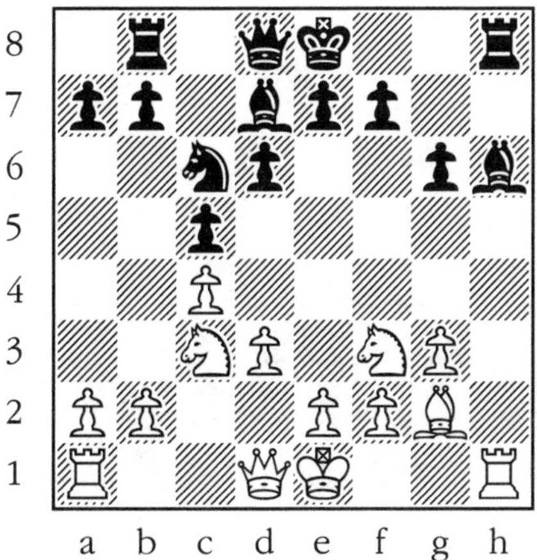

Diagram 46: White on move

11 Qd1-c1!!

A pin has unexpectedly popped up on the open h-file, and White exploits the pin with this stunning Queen move.

Of course, Black can't capture the Queen, as White would swoop down with Rh1xh8 checkmate. The real purpose of the move is to let the White Queen penetrate the Black position, eventually depriving Black of the right to castle.

11 ... Bh6-g7

The only move to avoid losing the Bishop.

12 Rh1xh8 check Bg7xh8
13 Qc1-h6!

White threatens Qc1xh8 checkmate. He's also hoping to bring his Knight into the attack at g5.

13 ... Bh8xc3 check

By capturing with check, Black buys himself a move to create some space around his King.

14 b2xc3

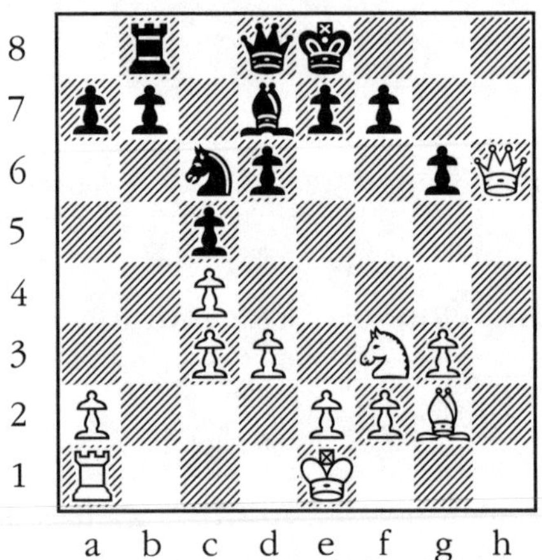

Diagram 47: Black to move

Black's next problem is to foil the threat of Qh6-h8 checkmate. Since he can't stop the Queen from getting to h8, he's going to have to move either the Bishop on d7 or the pawn on e7.

14 ... e7-e6!

The right way to handle the problem. Since the King's Rook is gone and the Queen's Rook has already moved, Black isn't going to be able to castle in this game. Black's going to have to create a secure spot for his King in the center. Black's move prepares to create that haven on e7.

CONCEDING A DRAW

A drawback to the e7 square is that White would have the option of taking a draw by perpetual check. In the present position for instance, White could check at h8, and Black would move his King to e7. White could then, if he wanted, check at h4, and Black would move back to e8. Since this process could continue forever, White could announce his intentions and eventually claim a draw by perpetual check.

Should Black be concerned about this outcome? No. If the game has started badly, a draw is sometimes the best you can do. At any rate, since it's White who has the initiative, it's unlikely that White will concede a draw just yet.

15 Nf3-g5

Adds to the pressure on the f7 square, giving Black something else to worry about.

BREAKING AN ATTACK

15 ... Ke8-e7!

This gives the King a little more security, and opens a new defensive resource for Black – the idea of playing Qd8-h8, followed by an exchange of Queens. If you're under a lot of pressure, one of the easiest ways to break the attack is through an exchange of pieces, especially the Queens. With fewer pieces on the board, the attacker is less able to generate threats.

16 Ke1-d2 Bd7-e8?

With this move Black misses the boat. The idea of Qd8-h8 was definitely the correct one, and after the exchange of Queens, Black would have no real problems drawing the game. Now

White begins to step up the pressure.

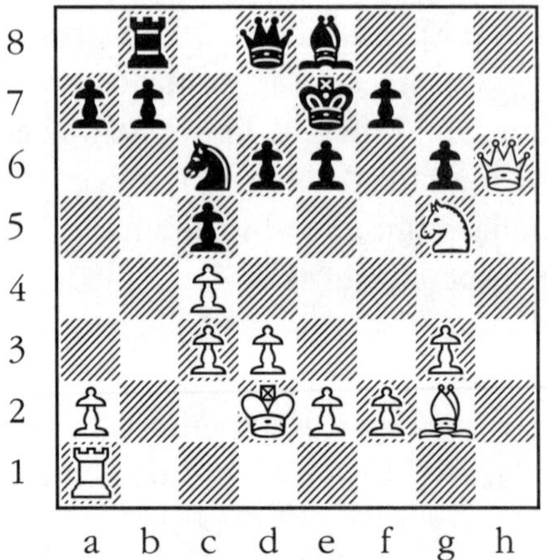

Diagram 48: White on move

17 Qh6-g7

White has no big threat, but rather a series of annoying smaller threats. Perhaps he'll play Ra1-h1-h8, or Ng5-h7 followed by Qg7-f8 check or Qg7-f6 check. When your opponent has one big threat, it's usually easy to see what to do: Find a defense or else. Against a series of smaller threats, the defender's task is sometimes more difficult. Are any of the threats really serious? Which one should I guard against? Should I ignore them and start an attack of my own? Questions like these aren't easily answered in the heat of battle, and the constant tension can wear a defender down.

17 ... Ke7-d7

Black decides the King would be safer on the Queen's side. He also sets a little trap. If White takes the offered pawn by Ng5xf7, Black pins the Knight with Qd8-e7, and captures it next turn.

18 f2-f4

Black was also threatening Qd8xg5 check. This guards the Knight and grabs a little more territory in the center.

18 ... Qd8-e7

This permanently guards the f-pawn. Black's King now seems pretty secure.

19 Ra1-h1

Now White threatens to penetrate the Rook into Black's position at either h7 or h8. Black is in some danger of getting completely tied up.

Notice how White is using his small threats to increase the activity of his pieces. Just compare the activity of the White and Black pieces right now. The White Rook occupies the only open file on the board, while the Black Rook squats uselessly behind its pawn. The White Queen controls the entire King-side from its fine post at g7, while the Black Queen is pinned to defense. The White Knight from g5 attacks e6 and f7, while the Black Knight is kept out of b4, d4, and e5, and can only move to a5 and e8. The White Bishop commands a beautiful diagonal from g2 to c6, but the Black Bishop on e8 has no moves at all!

The ability to use threats and subtle maneuvering to gradually increase one's control of the board is a skill characteristic of the greatest masters. As his control of the board increases, White can generate more threats while Black's defensive options begin to shrink. As Seigbert Tarrasch said almost a century ago, "A cramped position contains the seeds of defeat."

19 ... Nc6-d8

This beefs up the protection of f7 and e6. Unfortunately, Black's sphere of influence is steadily shrinking.

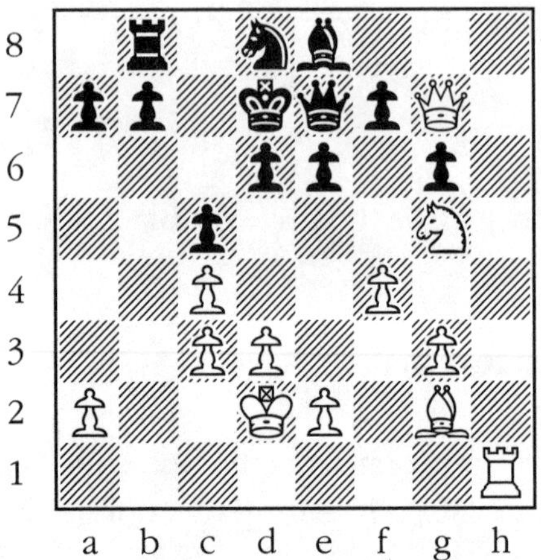

Diagram 49: White on move

20 Ng5-e4

The Knight was well placed on g5, but now it maneuvers its way to an even better square. Now a new threat is looming: Rh1-h8 (attacking the Bishop) followed by Ne4-f6 check, winning the Bishop. Black can defend against this threat, but White is continuing to make slow but steady progress.

20 ... Kd7-c7

This sidesteps the check and gives the Bishop an escape route on the diagonal e8-a4. With the King all the way over on the Queenside, surely it is safe from attack now.

21 Rh1-h8

Grabbing some more space. With the eighth rank firmly in White's hands, new threats will start to develop.

21 ... Be8-c6

Black would like to swap some of his passive pieces for White's active ones. Perhaps an upcoming Bc6xe4 will relieve some of the cramp.

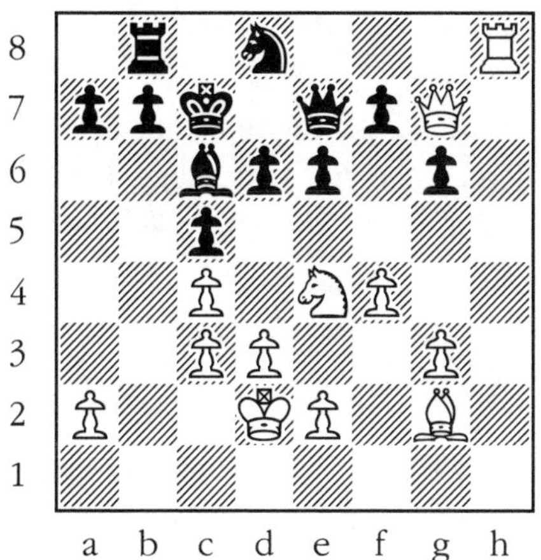

Diagram 50: White on move

22 Ne4-f6!!

White appears to be willing to sacrifice his Bishop on g2! Actually, it's not a real sacrifice. If Black is foolish enough to take the Bishop, White will play 23 Rh8-e8, trapping the Black Queen.

This isn't really a trap, since White knows that Black will not be foolish enough to take the Bishop, and as long as the Black Bishop remains at c6, White can't play Rh8-e8 without losing his Rook. What White is actually doing is continuing to squeeze Black back to the wall. White also has a number of small threats which must be dealt with. One possibility, for instance, is Rh8-f8, followed by Nf6-g8 and Ng8-h6, piling up on the weak pawn on f7. If that pawn goes, Black's position will collapse.

22 ... Kc7-b6

Black would like to find a nice safe haven for his King. Since White controls the whole of the center and the Kingside, Black decides his King will be safest on the Queenside. Besides, Black has hardly any moves left with the rest of his army. Right now, Black's King is his most mobile piece!

The real tactical point of the move is that the c7 square is now available to the Black Queen. Thus Black is really threatening to play Bc6xg2, and if White then plays Rh8-e8, Black can run away with Qe7-c7.

23 Bg2xc6

White's Bishop is now threatened. It has no good square to move to, so he exchanges it for Black's best piece.

23 ... Nd8xc6

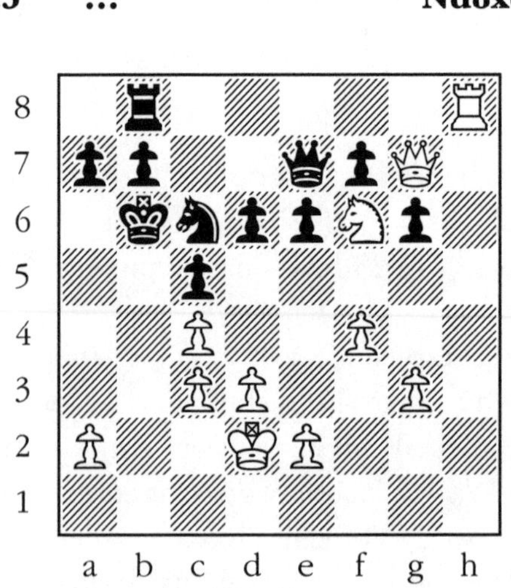

Diagram 51: White on move

24 Rh8-h7

White doesn't want to exchange his very active Rook for Black's very passive Rook. When you have more space and you're conducting an attack, you usually don't want to exchange pieces unless the exchange leads to a forced win. Instead you use your more active pieces to generate new threats.

On the last turn, White exchanged Bishops because he didn't have any real choice. Black's Bishop was just as active as White's (in fact it was Black's only active piece), and the only way to avoid an exchange was for White to retreat his own Bishop to a passive position, which of course wasn't a good idea.
Meanwhile White's Rook piles up pressure on the f-pawn. White now threatens Qg7xf7.

24 ... Nc6-d8

Back to defend the f-pawn. Why doesn't Black just defend the pawn by Rb8-f8, activating his Rook at the same time? Because White then has a neat little trap, based on a Knight fork: he plays 25 Qg7xf8! and after Qe7xf8, plays 26 Nf6-d7 check!, forking the Black King and the Black Queen.

In top-level plays, combinations such as this are hardly ever actually played out on the board. The opponent usually spots them and makes a different defensive move. (Your opponents, on the other hand, will often walk into these traps.) Grandmasters use the threat of these combinations to force their opponents to concede additional territory.

Unfortunately for Black, White had one additional threat, besides attacking the f-pawn. There was no way Black could guard against both threats, so his play of retreating the Knight was the best he had.

25 Qg7xg6!

White exploits the pin on the f-pawn, created by his Rook move last turn, to net his first piece of booty. (If Black plays f7xg6, White replies with Rh7xe7.) In addition, the absence of the g-pawn makes it easier for White's pieces to move over towards Black's King.

25 ... Kb6-a6

Black gets his King off the open b-file, to forestall a later attack by the White Rook. Black also threatens b7-b5, gaining some space for his Rook to get into the game. On a6, the King looks quite safe for now.

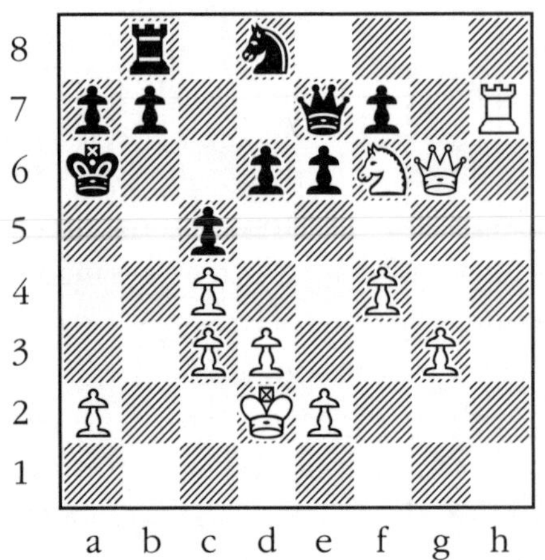

Diagram 52: White on move

26 a2-a4

All the members of White's army must be put to good use. The pawn adds an additional guard to the b5 square, preventing Black's contemplated freeing maneuver, b7-b5. But isn't the pawn itself a bit unguarded?

26 ... Ka6-a5

Black thinks so. The King itself steps up to pick off the pawn.

CREATING COUNTERCHANCES

Isn't this a bit dangerous? Of course. But what choices does Black have? Sitting still means that he will be a pawn down in an inferior position against a very strong player. That route will, in the long run, lead to certain defeat. Trying to win back the pawn might lose quickly, but it might also equalize the game if White doesn't respond properly.

If you're losing, you have to find ways to create counter-chances, even if it means taking risks you wouldn't take in an even position. Many a losing game has been saved through a courageous and unexpected counterattack.

Look at it another way. If you had a winning game with a little extra material, wouldn't you want your opponent to play passively? Of course you would. Then you could calmly figure out the easiest and best way to win. If your opponent complicates the position, even in a losing cause, there are more variations for you to calculate, and more chances of making a mistake. Black is making the best percentage play, even though it may (as it actually does in this game) lead to a quicker defeat.

27 Qg6-g5

This move frees the Rook, which otherwise had to stay where it was to keep the f7-pawn pinned.

27 ... Ka5xa4

Black eats the pawn, restoring material equality and giving himself a passed a-pawn. In addition, Black is ready to increase his Rook's mobility with b7-b5. The only drawback is that his King has become a tad exposed.

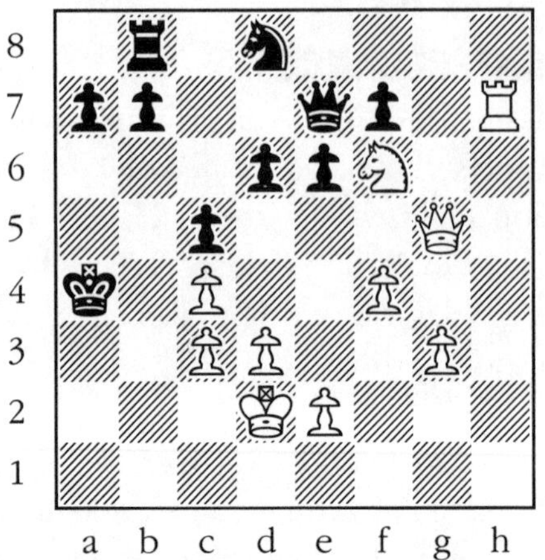

Diagram 53: White on move

28 Rh7-h1!

The Rook quickly relocates from the Kingside to the Queenside, preparing to attack the Black King.

Although the King would like to retreat, the avenues of escape have been cut off. The White pawns control the squares b4 and b5, while the square b6 has been indirectly controlled by White's move of the Queen to g5 three turns ago. Notice that if Black tries to escape via b6, the following variation would result: 28 ... Ka4-a5 29 Rh1-a1 check Ka5-b6, and now White would play 30 Nf6-d5 check!, attacking the King but also discovering an attack on Black's Queen from the White Queen at g5. Black could take the Knight, but White would reply Qg5xe7 with an easy win.

With all retreat cut off, Black's only possibility is to push forward.

28 ... Ka4-b3

If the King can reach b2, he may be able to keep the Rook from coming into play.

29 Qg5-h4

Now the Queen prepares to join in the attack by the route h4-h2-g1-a1.

29 ... Kb3-b2
30 g3-g4!

White's last move saves a little time by opening up a new attacking route for the White Queen via e1. Black resigns since he can't prevent mate by Qh4-e1, Qe1-a1, and Rh1-b1.

7

BACK-RANK MATE

The back-rank mate is the most common of the basic checkmates. It's based on a very simple idea. If Black's King is trapped on his first rank, hemmed in by his own pawns, and no pieces guard the first rank, then White can effect checkmate by moving a Rook or the Queen down to the first rank, giving check and checkmate at the same time. Here's a very simple example:

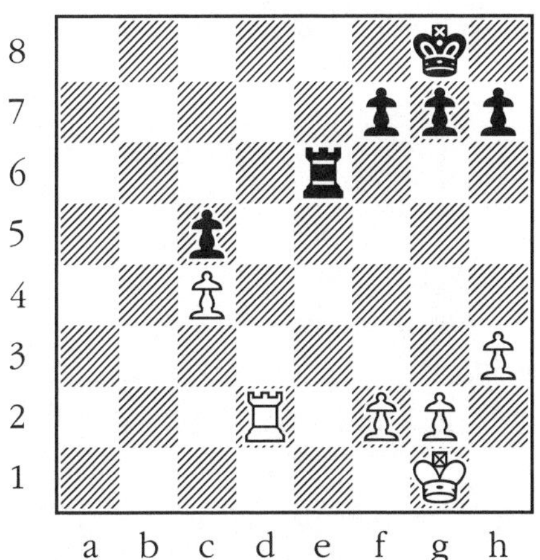

Diagram 54: White on move

White on move can force checkmate. He plays **1 Rd2-d8** check. Black's King is stuck behind his own pawns; the squares f8 and h8 are both under attack by the Rook. His only move to delay checkmate is the interposition move **1 ... Re6-e8.** White then finishes him off with **2 Rd8xe8 checkmate.**

Notice that if it had been Black's move instead of White's in Diagram 54, Black wouldn't have been able to checkmate White. If Black plays 1 ... Re6-e1 check, White's King can escape by Kg1-h2.

CREATING ESCAPE SQUARES

Creating an escape square for the King (also known as creating luft, from the German word for air) is often a good idea if done at just the right time. Moving the pawns in front of the King too early in the game can create addition attacking chances for the opponent. But later in the game, when the minor pieces are gone and the Queens and Rooks are roaming about, creating luft can be a very good idea.

CONDITIONS FOR A BACK RANK ATTACK

Mates as easy as the one in Diagram 54 won't simply appear over the board. Most players are aware of the possible weakness of the first rank and will make some effort to guard it. Most back-rank mating combinations that happen in real games are based on one of two situations:

1. One player is guarding his first rank with a Rook, but the Rook is guarding some other piece as well. The Rook is overworked: An attack on the piece it's guarding will either net some material or allow a back-rank checkmate.
2. The first rank is under attack but is guarded by some other pieces. If those pieces can be removed or harassed, the first rank will become vulnerable.

Most first rank combinations are based on one or both of these ideas. Let's look at a few examples.

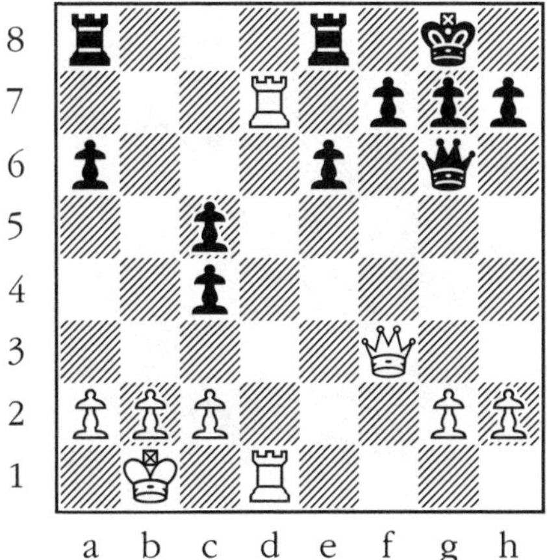

Diagram 55: White on move

Diagram 55 shows a typical back-rank attack in the middle game. Black's King is hemmed in by his pawns, but his first rank seems more than adequately guarded: It's protected by both of Black's Rooks. One of those Rooks is under attack, however, and that provides the key to White's winning combination.

White starts with **1 Qf3xa8!** Black recaptures, **Re8xa8.** Now only one Rook remains, while both White Rooks are aimed at the d8 square. White finishes with **2 Rd7-d8 check Ra8xd8 3 Rd1xd8 checkmate.**

A piece which can be knocked out of action in one turn isn't really an adequate defender.

Here's another example of that idea.

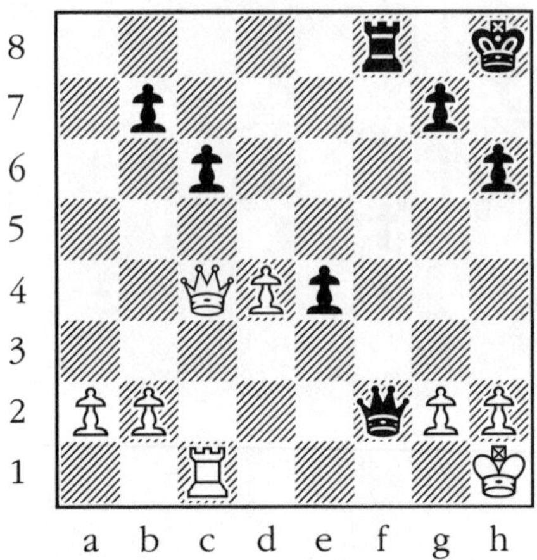

Diagram 56: Black on move

White's King is stuck in the corner, unable to move. If Black could penetrate to the f1 square with his Queen and Rook, he could deliver checkmate. Unfortunately, White guards this square quite adequately with his Rook on c1 and his Queen on c4. Can Black do something about one of these pieces?

In our last problem, the attacker was able to break through by capturing one of the guarding pieces. That's not a possibility here. But Black has a tactic that's equally good. He plays **1 ... b7-b5!**

The Black pawn attacks the Queen. The Queen has to continue to guard f1, otherwise Black will win with 2 ... Qf3-f1 check 3 Rc1xf1 Rf8xf1 mate. But where can the Queen go? The d3 square is guarded by Black's other pawn, while the e2 square is attacked by Black's Queen. If the Queen retreats to f1, Black simply snaps it off. There's no safe spot on the f1-b5 diagonal, so White has to resign.

CREATING BACK RANK WEAKNESSES

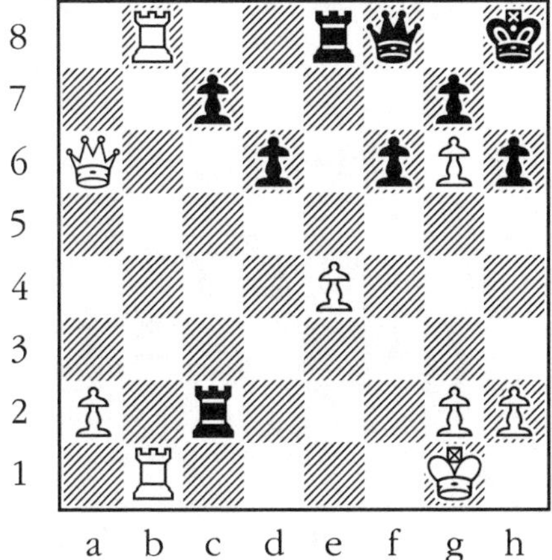

Diagram 57: White on move

In Diagram 57 the material is even, but White has an advantage in space. However, it's not easy at first to see how that translates into a winning attack. True, Black's King is confined to the first rank by a combination of his own pawns and White's pawn at g6. But the first rank seems well defended by the Rook and the Queen. In fact, Black has an immediate threat of 1 ... Re8xb8.

White's winning combination, however, is based on the weakness of that first rank. He starts with an exchange of Rooks: **1 Rb8xe8 Qf8xe8.** Now Black's defense of the first rank is in the hands of the Queen, who must stay there to prevent Rb1-b8 mate. Taking advantage of this fact, White plays a very unusual double attack. He plays **2 Qa6-a4!!**

The Queen attacks both the undefended Black Queen and the Black Rook. The White Queen is herself undefended, but that doesn't matter. Black can't leave the first rank to capture without being mated! Black must stay put and move the Queen along the rank, allowing White to take the Black Rook at c2.

A weakness along the first rank can render apparently powerful pieces powerless to operate. In this case the Black Queen doesn't really guard any squares off the first rank, and as a result the Rook is lost.

Let's look at another example of this theme:

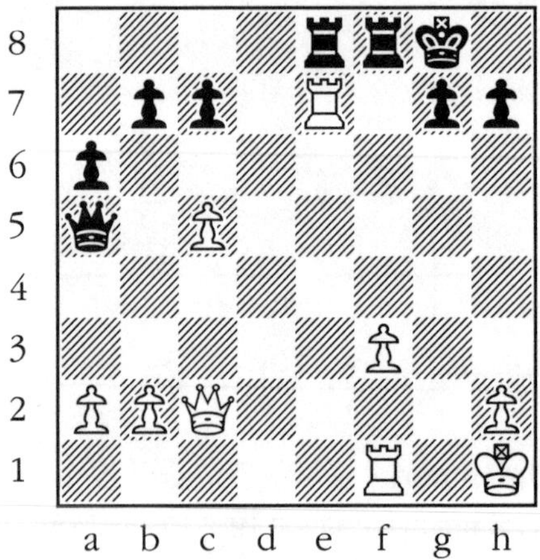

Diagram 58: White on move

In Diagram 58, there's no obvious weakness on the first rank yet. White could exchange Rooks by 1 Re7xe8 Rf8xe8, but that leaves Black's first rank well-guarded by the Black Rook. White needs to create some possibilities. He notices that he has a forcing check available, so he starts with **1 Qc2-c4 check.** Black's reply is forced. He plays **1 ... Kg8-h8.**

What has White accomplished with this check? Actually, a great deal. By driving the Black King into the corner, he has created more of a weakness on f8. Now the Black King no longer guards the Rook on that square. However, it takes a brilliant idea to exploit that weakness, and White is up to the task. He plays the logical but shocking **2 Qc4-f7!!**

Take a look at the next diagram.

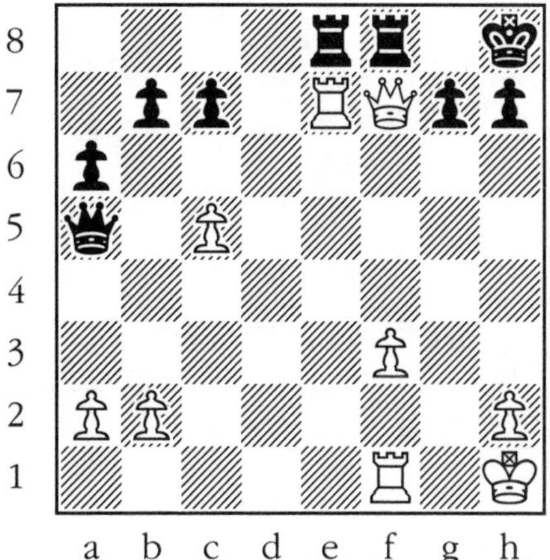

Diagram 59: Black on move

It's Black's turn, but what can he do? No matter which White piece he captures, the other will capture on the first rank, giving checkmate. If 2 ... Rf8xf7 3 Re7xe8 check, or if 2 ... Re8xe7 3 Qf7xf8 mate. In addition, White threatens 3 Qf7xg7 mate. If Black guards this by playing 2 ... Rf8-g8, White just plays 3 Re7xe8, winning easily. Black has to resign.

Notice the same idea as in the last position: Pieces that must guard the first rank don't really guard any other squares. In this case both Black Rooks were pinned to the rank and unable to move. The result – the f7 square was wide-open for White's Queen.

Sometimes a weakness on the first rank can be created by what appears to be an attacking move. In this case it may take an eagle eye and fantastic alertness to spot the flaw in the position.

Our next position is an amazing example of the possibilities against a weak first rank. Take a look.

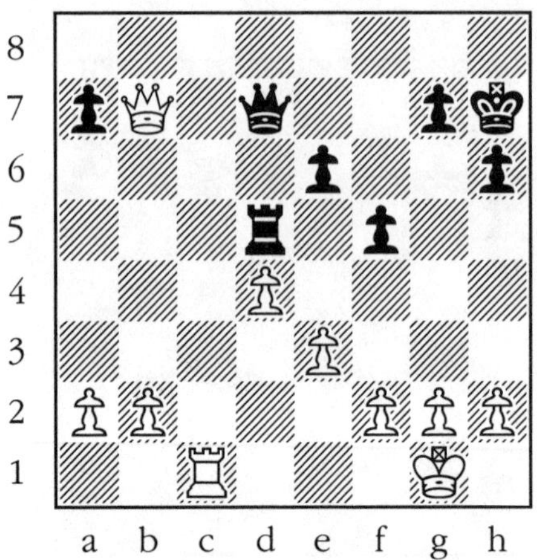

Diagram 60: White on move

In Diagram 60, White is two pawns ahead with an apparent simple win. His best course of action is the obvious 1 Qb7xd7 Rd5xd7. White would then be two pawns ahead in a Rook and pawn endgame. By centralizing his King and slowly advancing his extra pawns, White would have a sure but somewhat tedious win in his pocket.

On the other hand, why should White settle for a tedious win, when he has a very quick one available? White notices that if he plays his Rook down to c7, Black will be forced to move his Queen. White will then play Rc7xg7 check, with a checkmate in one or two more moves, for instance by Kh7-h8, Rg7-h7 check Kh8-g8, Qb7-g7. Against a threat like that, what can Black do except resign?

Confidently, White plays **1 Rc1-c7,** expecting Black to give up.

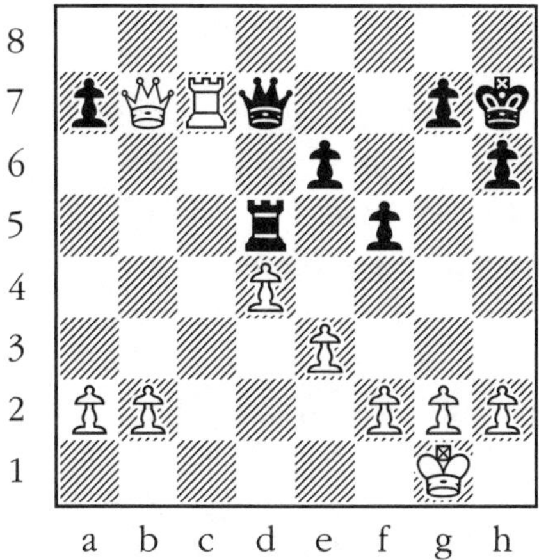

Diagram 61: Black on move

By moving the Rook away, White has removed the only defender of his first rank. "So what?" he thinks. "The rank may be vulnerable, but how can Black get to it? If he tries 1 ... Qd7-a4, threatening mate on d1, why I just checkmate him with 2 Rc7xg7 and so forth. The d-file is blocked, and I control the b-file and the c-file."

Sounds like good reasoning, but Black does have a move – one so amazing we can't really blame White for overlooking it. In Diagram 61, Black, instead of resigning, plays **1 ... Rd5-c5!!**

Incredible. Black's Rook and Queen are now both unprotected. White can take either piece, in several different ways. But look:

1. If White plays 2 Rc7xd7, Black responds with Rc5-c1 mate. That weak first rank!
2. If White plays 2 d4xc5, Black plays Qd7-d1 mate. Again the first rank weakness.
3. Finally, if White plays 2 Rc7xc5, Black plays Qd7xb7, with an advantage of a Queen for a Rook.

The last variation is the only one that lets White continue the game, but with a huge material advantage, Black is sure to win.

What made Black's combination so very hard to see was that it didn't begin with a check or a capture, the sort of forcing moves which begin most winning attacks. Instead, it started with an odd-looking move which just left all Black's pieces unguarded! Such moves are very tricky to see over the board.

You have to train yourself to look for them.

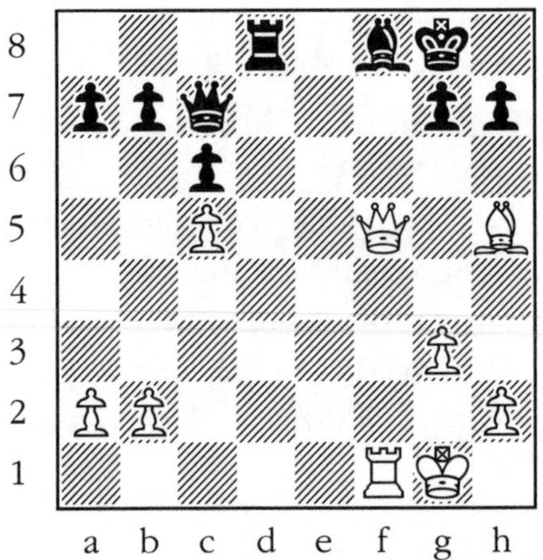

Diagram 62: White on move

In Diagram 62 White has an advantage, but he must be careful about how he proceeds. The Bishop at f8 is well-protected, so White can't capture it. Penetrating to the seventh rank with the Queen doesn't accomplish anything. If White tries 1 Qf5-f7 check Qc7xf7 2 Rf1xf7, Black has the simple refutation 2 ... g7-g6! and both White's Bishop and Rook are under simultaneous attack. The other check with the Queen, 1 Qf5-e6 check, also doesn't lead anywhere after 1 ... Kg8-h8.

White does, however, have a winning attack. He begins by creating a weakness on the last rank. He plays **1 Bh5-f7 check!** Black naturally responds with **1 ... Kg8-h8.**

With his check, White has managed to both chase the King into the corner and simultaneously remove a defender from the Bishop on f8. But what can he do about the weakness? If he retreats the Bishop with something like 2 Bf7-b3, threatening 3 Qf5xf8 check and mate next, Black can defend by simply playing Qc7-e7. Clearly White needs a Bishop move which also involves some other threat.

White finds the answer with **2 Bf7-e8!!** This outstanding move is an example of an attacking idea we haven't seen before: an interference move. The Bishop uncovers the Queen's attack on f8 and at the same time interferes with the Black Rook's defense of f8. Suddenly the Bishop is attacked twice and completely undefended.

What can Black do? Taking the White Bishop allows 3 Qf5xf8 check and mate next move. Moving the Bishop allows 3 Qf5-f8 check with the same result. And defending the Bishop with the Queen also allows White to take it off and follow up with mate. Black has to resign.

INTERFERENCE

Interference is a way of cutting communication between the opposing forces. In this problem, Black's first rank was defended by the line of communication between the Rook and the Bishop. When White cut the line by B-e8, he in effect created a double attack on the Bishop where none had existed before. Interference is a very powerful attacking idea, though not one of the most common.

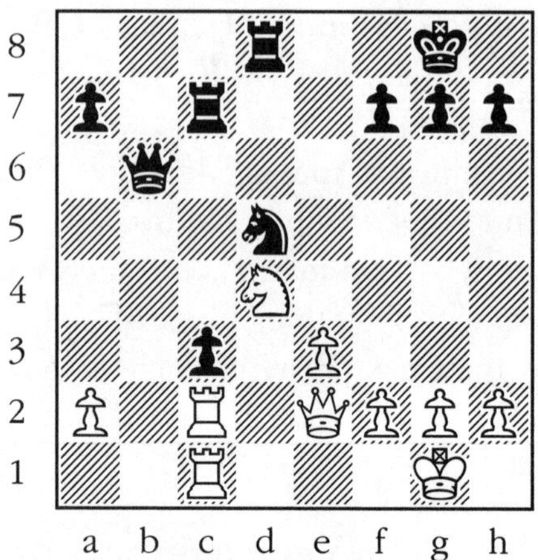

Diagram 63: White on move

In some cases, threats against the back rank are not really part of an attack, but can serve as a defensive resource. One side may not be able to pursue its long range plans because of a latent weakness on the back rank.

Take a look at Position 63. The material is even, but Black has an advanced pawn which severely cramps White's game.

Obviously White would like to eliminate the pawn if he could. But can he? White sees a combination which appears to win the pawn, based, curiously enough, on the weakness of Black's first rank. But Black sees a bit farther, and notices that the combination will not work, based on the weakness of White's first rank!

Let's take a look at the play.

White starts with a Knight fork. He plays **1 Nd4-b5,** simultaneously attacking the Black Rook on c7 while adding a third attacker to the pawn on c3. He thinks: "Black will have to move the Rook, and then I'll pick off the pawn, since I attack it three times and Black only defends it twice." This reasoning is correct, as far as it goes.

Sure enough, Black moves the Rook, **1 ... Rc7-c5.** Now comes the exchange of pieces that White has foreseen: **2 Nb5xc3 Nd5xc3 3 Rc2xc3 Rc5xc3 4 Rc1xc3.**

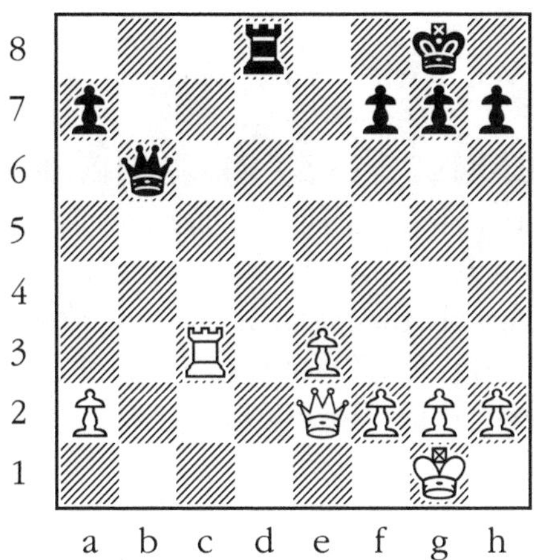

Diagram 64: Black on move

Take a look. White has successfully captured the Black pawn. Although Black can penetrate to White's first rank with 4 ... Qb6-b1 check, White has prepared a very clever defense: 5 Qe2-f1! and if Black follows up with Rd8-d1, White turns the tables with 6 Rc3-c8 check! and mate comes next turn.

So White wins, right? That's what White thought. Unfortunately, Black had seen much farther ahead. Back in the position of our first diagram, Black had foreseen this exact position and realized that he had a much deadlier threat than the crude Qb6-b1. Instead, he plays the ingenious **4 ... Qb6-b2!!**

Now what?

If White takes the Queen, 5 Qe2xb2, Black swoops down with Rd8-d1 checkmate. Meanwhile, both the White Queen and the White Rook are under attack. If the Queen moves to defend the Rook, 5 Qe2-e1, Black plays Qb2xc3 and then Rd8-d1. If the Rook blocks the attack with 5 Rc3-c2, Black now plays Qb2-b1 check! The difference from before is that now when White blocks with 6 Qe2-f1, Black has Qb1xc2, emerging a Rook ahead.

No matter what White tries, Black wins at least a Rook.

DEFENDING AGAINST A LAST RANK THREAT

The easiest way to defend against attacks on the back rank is to create luft for your King, by moving one of the pawns in front of the King (preferably the h-pawn) at some point in the game. Keep in mind that this may create an object of attack, as we saw in earlier chapters, so you have to be very careful in assessing the possibilities.

Remember that if the center files are closed, there's usually no serious danger of a back rank mate, so you may want to leave your pawns alone until later.

Also remember that not all attacks against the back rank are sound. If you can calculate the possibilities accurately, you may be able to use an apparent weakness on the back rank as a trap. Take a look at the following position.

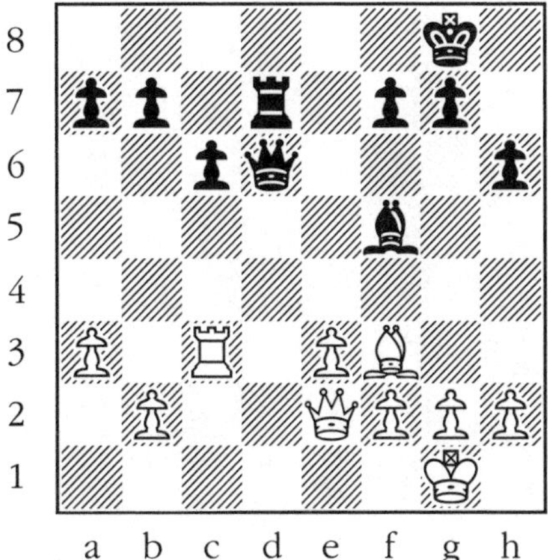

Diagram 65: White to move

In Diagram 65, White would like to play e3-e4, pushing the Black Bishop away and gaining more control of the center. White must be careful, however. Black controls the d-file and White's King has no escape squares, so there might be some danger of a back rank combination.

White does the calculations and sees that if Black tries to win on the back rank, White will have a defense. So he correctly plays **1 e3-e4!**

Black thinks this move loses a pawn or walks into mate, because both White's Queen and Bishop are needed for defense of the d1 square. So he plays what he thinks is a winning combination: **1 ... Bf5xe4?**

White captures (falling into Black's trap) with **2 Bf3xe4,** and Black swoops down with **2 ... Qd6-d1 check,** expecting White to resign, since if he plays 3 Qe2xd1, Black has Rd7xd1 checkmate.

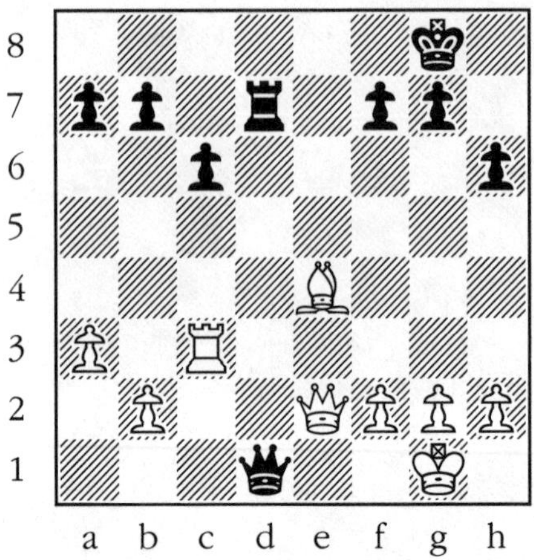

Diagram 66: Black has played 2 ... Qd6-d1 check. White to move.

But White doesn't resign. Instead, he just retreats: **3 Qe2-f1!,** and suddenly it's Black who is just a piece down with no attack. (If Black plays 3 ... Qd1xf1 check 4 Kg1xf1 Rd7-d1 check, White just steps out with 5 Kf1-e2.) If a defensive piece has access to the f1 square, a back rank attack may well fail.

8

THE SMOTHERED MATE

The Knight is a special piece with a special kind of move. Unlike other pieces, it moves by hopping over pieces to the squares beyond.

Just as the Knight has a special kind of move, so there is also a special kind of mating attack based on the Knight's move. It's called a smothered mate, and it occurs when the enemy King is trapped by his own pieces, then attacked by a Knight which cannot be captured. If a King is completely hemmed in, a Knight check may in fact be all that's required to give mate.

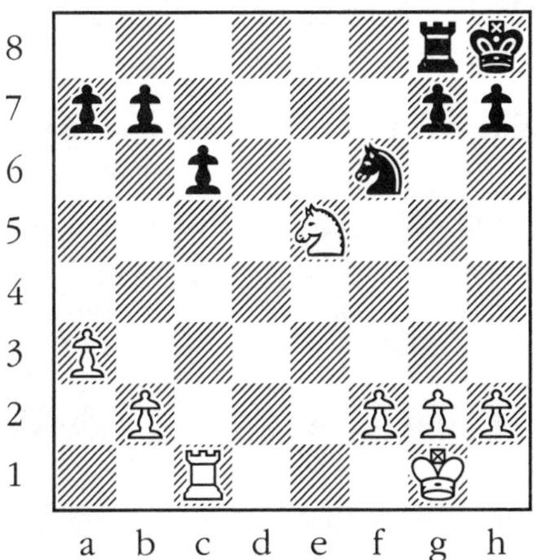

Diagram 67: White on move

Diagram 67 shows the basic pattern of the smothered mate. Black's King is trapped in the corner, blocked from moving by its pawns and Rook. White plays **1 Ne5-f7 checkmate.** The King can't move, and no piece can block a Knight's check. Offhand, it looks like Black has played very badly to be mated in Diagram 67. Let's now look at a more typical smothered mating combination, as it might arise in an actual game.

BASIC SMOTHERED MATE PATTERN

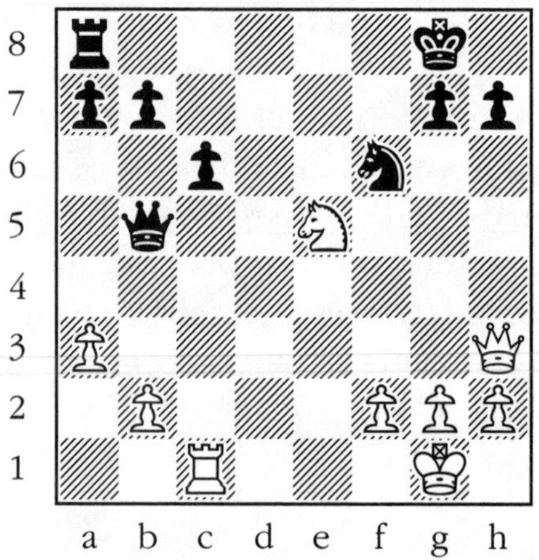

Diagram 68: White on move

Although it might appear that White just has a few checks in Diagram 68, he actually has a forced mate in five moves! Here's how the sequence would go:

1 Qh3-e6 check Kg8-h8

If Black plays instead Kg8-f8, White has Qe6-f7 mate.

2 Ne5-f7 check! Kh8-g8

Forced.

3 Nf7-h6 double check! Kg8-h8

The only response to a double check is to move the King. As before, Black gets mated if he goes to f8. But now follows

4 Qe6-g8 check!! Ra8xg8

Taking with the Black Knight leads to the same result.

5 Nh6-f7 checkmate

The smothered mate was set up by sacrificing the Queen, forcing one of the Black pieces to block its own King. Memorize the pattern in Diagram 68; you'll find many opportunities to use it, or some variation, in your actual games.

Here's a similar example, where the defender of the f7-square is lured away by another mating threat:

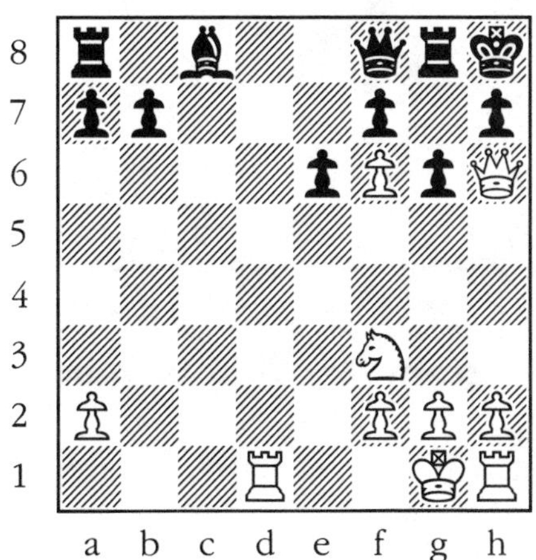

Diagram 69: White on move

Black has just played his Queen back to f8 to offer an exchange of Queens. White could agree to this swap, but in that case he'd be a pawn down, with just some extra piece activity to compensate. Instead, he decides to checkmate in two moves!

White plays **1 Nf3-g5!!,** threatening Qh6xh7 checkmate. Black doesn't have much choice, since the White pawn prevents any pieces from going to g7. He takes the offered Queen by **1 ... Qf8xh6.** White ends the game with **2 Ng5xf7 mate.**

SMOTHERED KING IN THE CENTER

The enemy King doesn't need to be trapped in the corner. A King can be "smothered" anywhere on the board so long as his own pieces have got in the way and a Knight can hop somewhere to deliver the fatal blow.

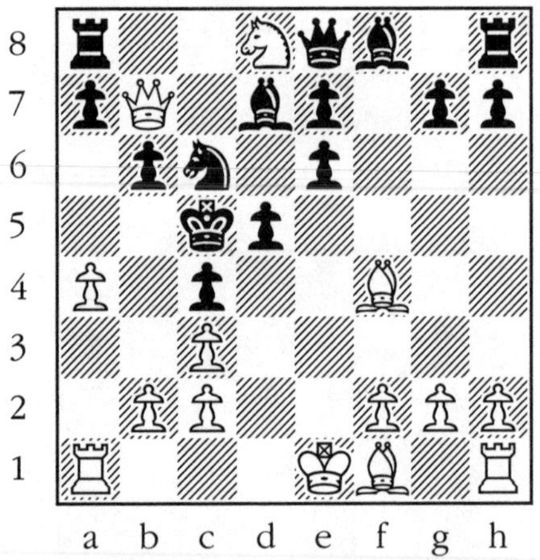

Diagram 70: White on move

White's pieces have infiltrated the Black position and Black's King has been driven into the center of the board, as in the King hunts we studied earlier. Now Black's King is completely immobilized. But how does White deliver checkmate? If he tries 1 Bf4-e3 check, Black just retreats with 1 ... Kc5-d6, and his position is even safer than before.

When the enemy King is in trouble, look around for moves which would be checkmate if some feature of the position were different. Then see if you can change that feature.

White notices that Nd8xe6 would be checkmate, that is, if Black Bishop didn't guard e6. And Qb7xc6 would be checkmate, if the Black Bishop didn't guard c6. As we see, the Black Bishop seems to have two critical jobs, and that's one job too many.

White exploits the Bishop's situation with the right sequence of forcing moves: **1 Qb7xc6 check!! Bd7xc6 2 Nd8xe6 checkmate.** A smothered mate in the middle of the board!

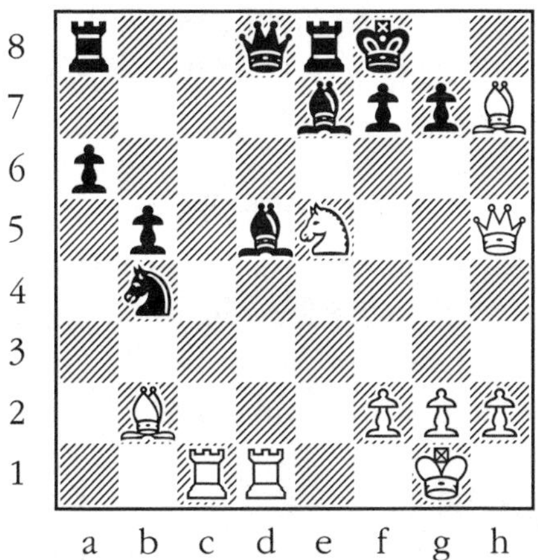

Diagram 71: White on move

In Diagram 71 White seems to have the potential for a winning attack, but the finishing touch is difficult to locate. White would like to play 1 Qh5xf7, but the Bishop on d5 guards that square. Then White notices that the Black King is completely immobilized, so a check by his Knight could be mate. Unfortunately, Black guards all the key squares: Ne5-g6 check is answered by f7xg6, while Ne5-d7 check is repulsed by Qd8xd7.

White could eliminate the Black Queen's guard on d7 by sacrificing his own Queen first. If he played 1 Qh5xf7 check Bd5xf7 2 Rd1xd8, the Black Queen is gone. But Black just plays 2 ... Ra8xd8, and the Rook takes over the Queen's job of defending d7.

Is there a way to break through? Yes! But it requires making some substitutions in the Black defensive lineup. White starts with **1 Rd1xd5!** Black replies **1 ... Qd8xd5.** (If the Knight captures, White has 2 Qh5xf7 mate.)

What has White accomplished by replacing the Bishop with the Queen? He's created an overworked piece. The Queen now has two jobs: she has to stop the checkmate on f7 as well as the checkmate on d7. That's one job too many. White now finishes his masterpiece with the sequence **2 Qh5xf7 check!! Qd5xf7 3 Ne5-d7 mate!**

SMOTHERED MATE IN THE OPENING

On occasion, one side can effect a smothered mate right in the opening. Take a look at the following game, played between the former World Champion Alexander Alekhine (White) and a team of four amateurs consulting as Black.

	ALEKHINE	**FOURAMATEURS**
1	**e2-e4**	**c7-c6**

This is the Caro-Kann defense, named after the players Caro and Kann, who formed it into a real system. Black's idea is to contest the center with d7-d5 next turn, while keeping the diagonal free for the Bishop at c8 to get into the game. It's a super-solid defense, favored by players who like endgames and simple positions.

2	**d2-d4**	**d7-d5**
3	**Nb1-c3**	**d5xe4**

4 Nc3xe4 Nb8-d7

Black could play 4 ... Ng8-f6, but this would allow White to double his pawns by 5 Ne4xf6 check. That wouldn't be fatal for Black, but he's trying to avoid doubled pawns, so he prepares to recapture with his other Knight.

5 Qd1-e2

This prevents Black from developing the other Knight.

5 ... Ng8-f6??

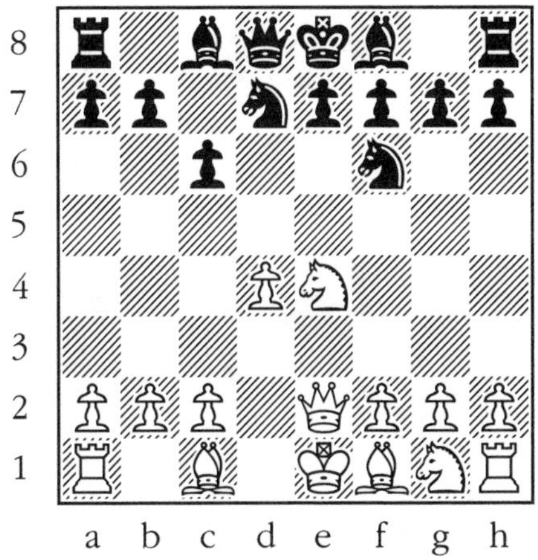

Diagram 72: Black has played Ng8-f6

The four amateurs don't notice that this move was prevented. Black should have played e7-e6 or Nd7-f6.

6 Ne4-d6 checkmate!

Oops. The Knight wasn't headed for f6 after all.

9

MATE WITH TWO KNIGHTS

If a single Knight can be such a powerful checkmating tool, how about two Knights?

Two Knights can be a very strong attacking force, particularly in close quarters where there are no open files for the Rooks and the enemy King seems well defended by pawns. Knights don't need open lines or files and have no regard for a defensive pawn block. Under the X-ray attack of a couple of Knights, pawns can become obstacles for the King's escape rather than staunch defenders.

USING THE QUEEN

Knights are even stronger when combined with the attacking power of the Queen, who often provides the means to construct the actual mating position. When a Queen and two Knights have penetrated near the enemy King, follow this rule: Look at all checks and captures, even those which seem absurd at first glance.

A Queen sacrifice can often rearrange the defensive pieces in a way that will allow the Knights to finish off the King.

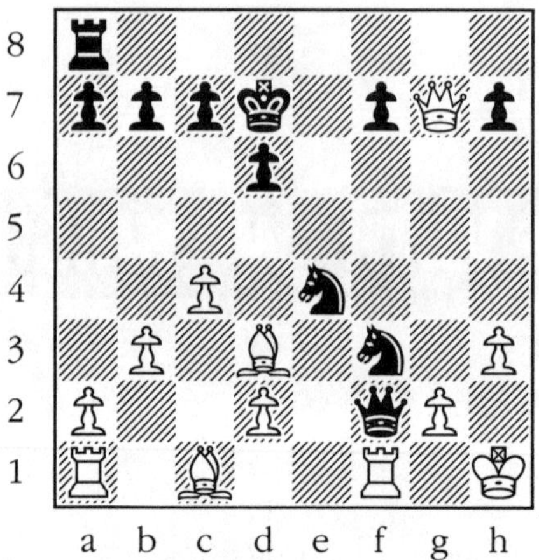

Diagram 73: Black on move

Black has sacrificed a Rook to reach Position 73. At first glance, White's defensive resources seems adequate. The Rook attacks the Queen and also the Knight behind the Queen. White's Bishop is ready to pick off the other Black Knight. Black can win White's Queen with the sequence 1 ... Ne4-g3 check 2 Qg7xg3 Qf2xg3, but then White plays 3 Rf1xf3, and has a solid material advantage of a Rook and two Bishops for the Queen.

Black needs something a bit better, and he needs it immediately. Fortunately the power of the two Knights provides the answer.

Black plays **1 ... Qf2-g1 check!!** White has to capture, **2 Rf1xg1,** and then Black has the elegant **Ne4-f2 mate!** The Queen sacrifice bottled the King in the corner, after which the leaping ability of the Knights made White's defensive barrier useless.

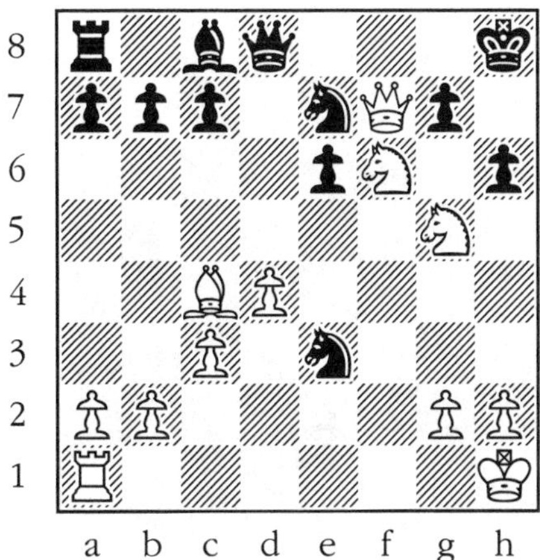

Diagram 74: White on move

Diagram 74 shows a variation on that same idea. It would now be a mistake for White to sacrifice his Queen by 1 Qf7-g8 check. True, this would lead to mate as in the last problem if Black blundered with 1 ... Ne7xg8, since then White would have 2 Ng5-f7 mate. However, Black should simply play 1 ... Qd8xg8! after which White wouldn't have anything.

There is a way to break through, but White must try something a little different. He has to clear the f7-square, while not allowing Black time for a defense. The right idea is **1 Qf7-g6!!** The Queen moves aside and threatens mate at h7. Black can take either Knight, but the remaining Knight would still back up the Queen. And if Black plays 1 ... Ne7xg6, White mates with 2 Ng5-f7.

COORDINATING THE KNIGHTS

Black seems to have a strong attack in Diagram 75, but so does White. If Black tries the obvious continuation, 1 ... Qh5-h3, threatening Qh3-g2 mate, his threat comes one move too late. As soon as the Black Queen moves away from the e8-h5 diagonal, White can play 2 Qb5-e8 mate. If Black tries to block the Queen's attack with c7-c6, White has the comfortable choice between 2 Qb5xe5 or 2 Qb5xb7 check.

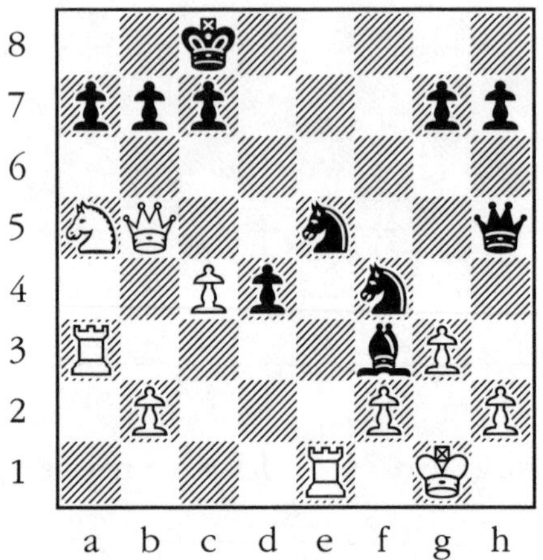

Diagram 75: Black on move

It looks like Black's attack is one move too slow, but he has a way to push it home. The winning idea shows the remarkable power of the Knights in confined, blocked positions.

Black starts with a check: **1 ... Qh5xh2 check!!** White has to capture, **2 Kg1xh2.** Now Black plays **2 ... Ne5-g4 check.** White has no choice; he must retreat, **3 Kh2-g1.**

Now Black plays **3 ... Nf4-h3 check.** Again White has only one move, **4 Kg1-f1.** Black winds up with **4 ... Ng4-h2 mate!** With just a limited amount of space, the Knights are ideal pieces to conduct an attack.

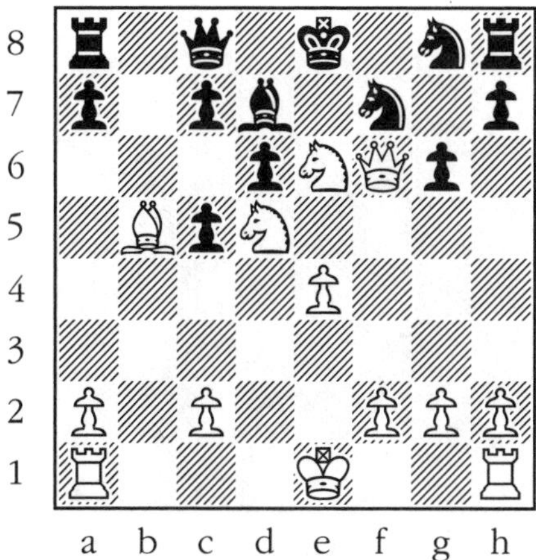

Diagram 76: White on move

White has a roaring attack in Diagram 76, but Black seems to have all the vital squares covered for the moment. With two Knights and a Queen on the rampage, however, White follows a basic rule: examine all checks and captures. As he does, White discovers a mate in just two moves: **1 Qf6-e7 check!! Ng8xe7 2 Nd5-f6 mate!**

This is a basic mating pattern with the two Knights.

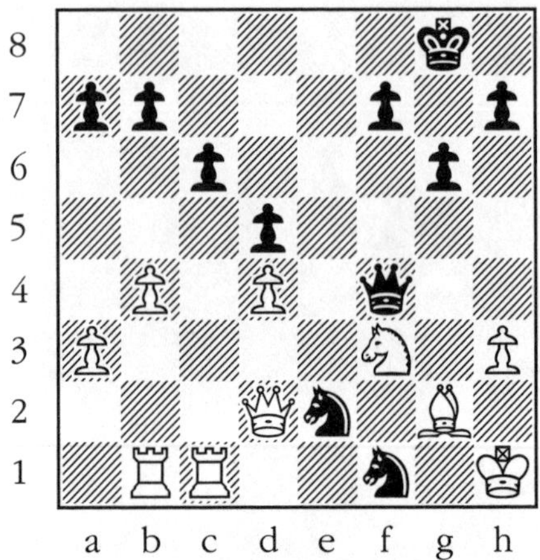

Diagram 77: Black on move

Black has sacrificed two Rooks to get to Position 77, because he knew he could force a checkmate in two moves. The pattern is slightly different from Position 76: **1 ... Qf4-h2 check! 2 Nf3xh2 Nf1-g3 mate.** Once again, White's own pieces are forced to block his King, and the Knights are able to finish the job.

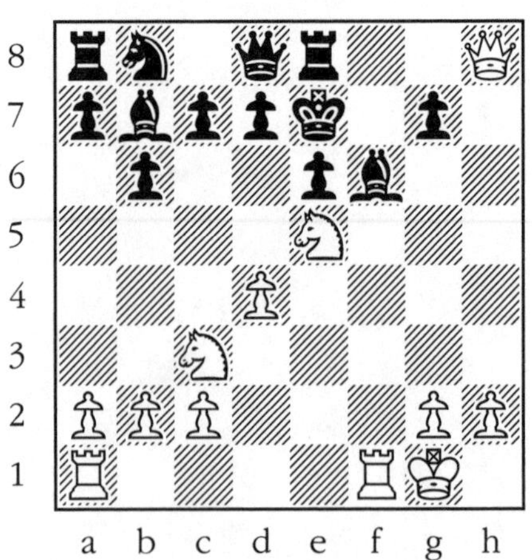

Diagram 78: White on move

The last attack in this chapter shows a King hunt conducted mostly by the Knights. Take a look as White breaks through Black's defenses.

White starts by sacrificing his Queen to get the Rook into the game: **1 Qh8xg7 check!! Bf6xg7 2 Rf1-f7 check Ke7-d6.** The King move was forced.

Now the Knights strut their stuff: **3 Nc3-b5 check! Kd6-d5 4 c2-c4 check!** Take a look. The Knights cooperate beautifully, cutting off the c6 and d6 squares while simultaneously guarding the pawns on c4 and d4, which in turn do their part by guarding the Knights! Black only has **4 ... Kd5-e4,** when White finishes with **5 Ra1-e1 mate!** A brilliant example of harmonious cooperation between the minor pieces.

10

THE CORRIDOR MATE

The easiest place to checkmate the enemy King is in the corner or along the sides of the board. That's because the edge of the board does part of the work for you. A King on the edge has at most five squares to which he could legally move, rather than his usual eight. That's fewer squares for the attacker to cover, hence fewer pieces needed to administer the mate.

We've already seen an example of this in the back rank mate, where frequently a single Rook, operating along the back rank, was sufficient for checkmate. The corridor mate is a variation of the back rank mate, except, instead of occurring along the back edge of the board, the mate takes place along one of the side files (usually the h-file, since most Kings are castled on the King-side in the early game.)

THE TWO STAGES OF A CORRIDOR MATE

A corridor mate usually occurs in two stages: first the King is separated from the defending pieces, often by means of a Queen sacrifice. Then the King is hunted down and trapped on the side of the board. In the corridor mate, the key pieces are usually the Bishops and Knights, rather than the Rook, since the h-file is often blocked from the attacker's side by a pawn.

Let's take a look at an example of the corridor mate:

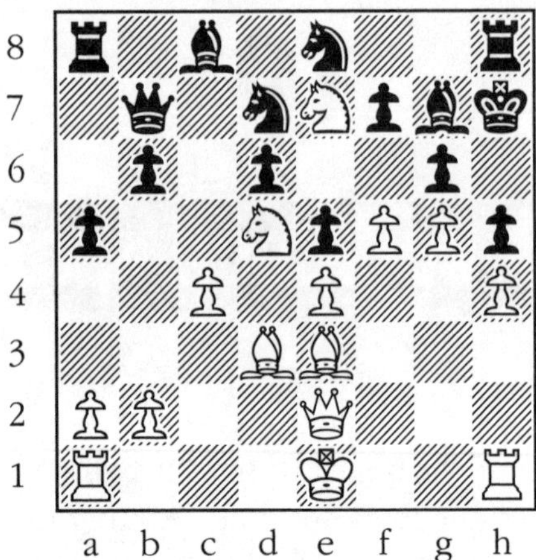

Diagram 79: White on move

White has a huge advantage in space in Problem 79, with Black's pieces clustered at the edges of the board. That's a sure sign that a winning attack is looming on the horizon.

Most important, Black's King is confined to the h-file by its own Bishop and the White Knight on e7. If only White could get at the King, it wouldn't take much to effect a checkmate. After some thought, White spots the way.

He starts with a simple exchange of pawns: **1 f5xg6 check f7xg6.** His next move isn't quite so simple. White sacrifices his Queen with **2 Qe2xh5 check!!** Black has to play **g6xh5.**

Why did White give up his Queen? To clear the way for the pawn on g5 to advance! White finishes his attack with **3 g5-g6 mate.** The White Knight and the Black Bishop keep the King confined to the h-file, the Bishop on e3 guards h6, while the pawn on g6 gives mate.

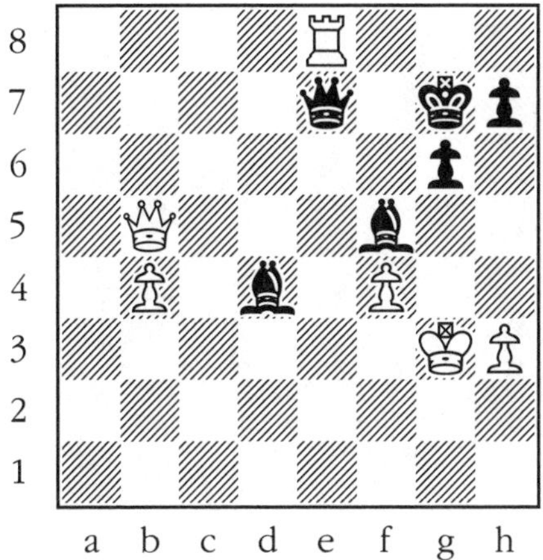

Diagram 80: Black to move

On a wide-open board, White has Rook and pawn against Black's two Bishops, about an even material situation. But it's Black's move, and that means that Black can strike the first blow, if he can find a way.

White's King, however, looks rather safe for the moment. White's Rook guards the e-file, so Black can't penetrate with his Queen that way. The Bishop check at f2 looks like a waste of time. Is there any other way to proceed? Black follows the rule of examining all checks and captures, even the most silly-looking, and comes up with an idea.

He plays 1 ... **Qe7-h4 check!!** White has to capture, since otherwise Black will check at f2 next turn with a quick mate. So he plays **2 Kg3xh4**. Now Black has **2 ... Bd4-f2 check!** The White King on the h-file suddenly has very few options. He must flee with **3 Kh4-g5.** Now he has no moves at all, so any good check will do the trick. Black plays **3 ... h7-h6 mate!**

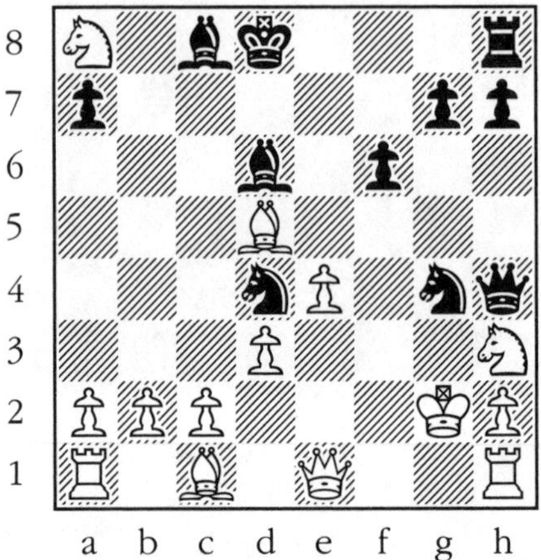

Diagram 81: Black on move

In Diagram 81, Black has sacrificed a Rook and two pawns for a roaring attack. But can he bring the attack home? White has just moved Qd1-e1, offering to trade Queens, which would break the back of Black's attack. How does Black proceed? He could exchange Queens and then play Nd4xc2, which would win back some, but not all, of his lost material. But can he do better?

"Certainly!" says Black.

He plays **1 ... Qh4xh3 check!!** Unwilling to trade Queens, he simply gives up his Queen for a Knight. White plays **2 Kg2xh3.** Now Black replies **2 ... Ng4-e3 discovered check!**

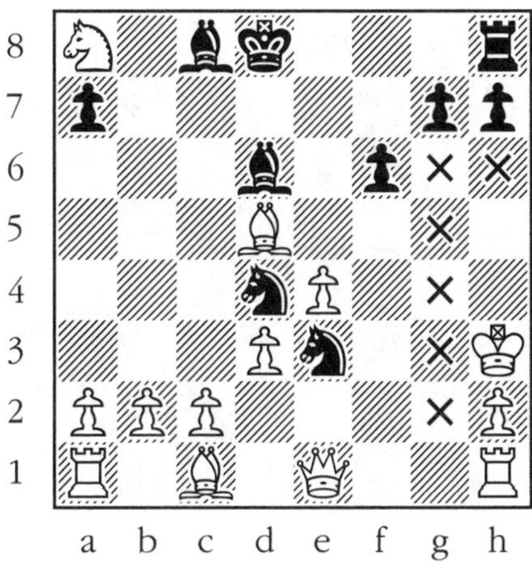

Diagram 82: Black has played Ng4-e3 check

This move was the real point of Black's play. The Knight uncovers an attack on the King by the Bishop at c8. Take a look at diagram 82, and notice how the Black pieces have set up a wall around the White King. The Knight controls g4 and g2, the Bishop on d6 controls g3, and the Black pawns control g5, g6, and h6. The White King is locked in the corridor from h3 to h5, and Black should have enough material to mate him there.

The finish is easy. White plays **3 Kh3-h4,** and Black mates with **3 ... Nd4-f3 check 4 Kh4-h5 Bc8-g4 mate.**

The next position is from one of my own games. (Unfortunately, I was on the losing side!)

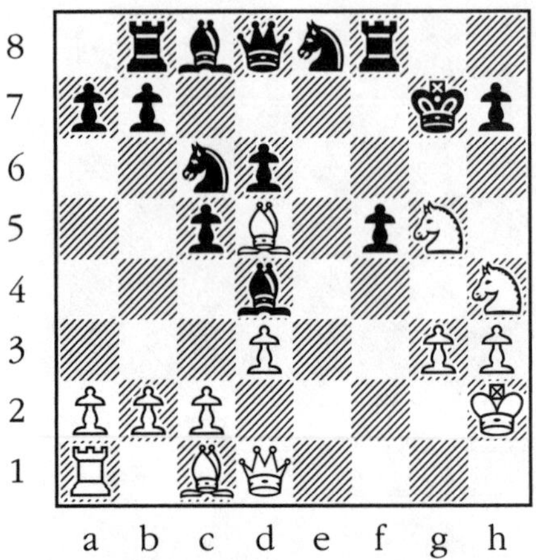

Diagram 83: White on move

White has sacrificed a Rook to mobilize his minor pieces and expose Black's King. He begins the final phase of his attack by bringing up the heavy artillery. He plays **1 Qd1-h5**, threatening (among other things) 2 Qh5xh7 check.

Black has several ways to defend against this threat, most of which clearly fail. He could try 1 ... h7-h6, moving the pawn to a protected square, but then White sneaks in with 2 Qh5-g6 check, and after Kg7-h8, he has 3 Qg6xh6 mate.

Black could also defend the pawn with the Rook, 1 ... Rf8-h8, but then White wins with 2 Qh5-f7 check Kg7-h6 3 Ng5-e6 discovered check Qd8-g5 4 Bc1xg5 mate.

However, Black has a defense which looks perfectly good at first glance. He moves **1 ... Ne8-f6**, guarding the h-pawn and counterattacking the Queen. If the Queen retreats, say to f3, Black would play Nc6-e5, counterattacking again and driving White further back, leaving Black with an extra Rook. This defense looks strong, and in fact Black was counting on it to win the game.

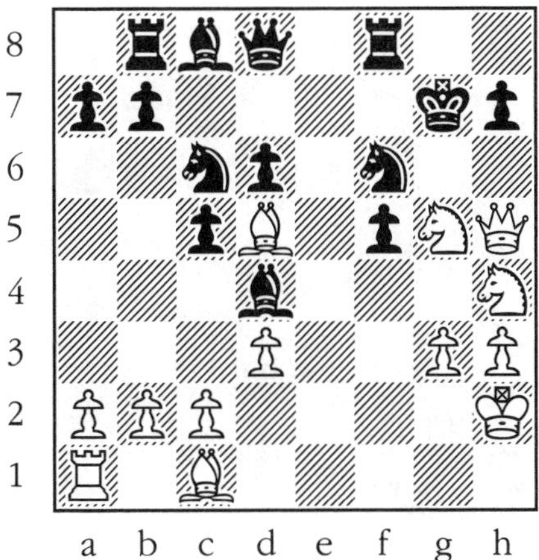

Diagram 84: Black has played 1 ... Ne8-f6

Unfortunately for Black, White has seen farther and now executes a beautiful h-file corridor mate.

He starts with **2 Qh5-h6 check!!** Black certainly didn't expect this. If he tries to escape with 2 ... Kg7-h8, White has 3 Nh4-g6 mate, so Black grimly takes the Queen: **2 ... Kg7xh6.** Now White plays **3 Ng5-e6 discovered check!**

This move would win back the Queen, but that's not White's intention. Notice that the Knight on e6 covers g7 and g5, while the Knight on h4 covers g6. As in our previous examples, the Black King is cut off from retreat and has to shuffle forward along the h-file. Black plays **3 ... Kh6-h5**.

The end is quick and simple. White just plays **4 Ne6-g7 mate**. (The winner of this elegant game, by the way, was the great New England master John Curdo.)

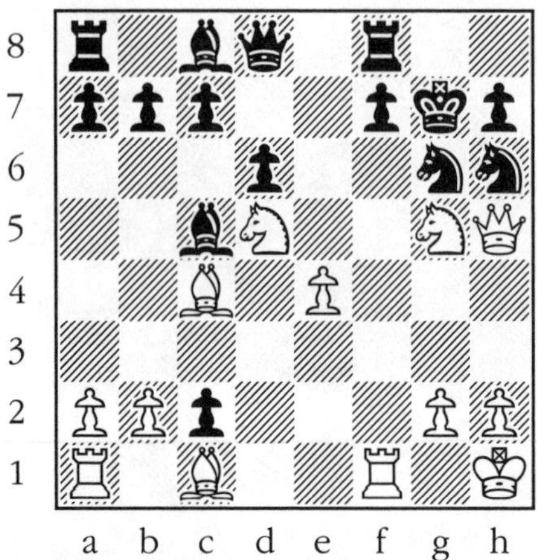

Diagram 85: White on move

Problem 85 shows a variation on the same theme. White has a powerful attack with his Queen and all his minor pieces in play. In addition, his Rook controls the open f-file.

After the previous examples, you should be able to spot the key moves of a potential corridor mate: White starts with **1 Qh5xh6 check!** Black must take the Queen, since otherwise White will play 2 Qh6xh7 mate. So he plays **1 ... Kg7xh6.** Now White has a discovered check, **2 Ng5-e6 discovered check Kh6-h5**. White brings his white-squared Bishop into play, at the same time cutting Black's last line of escape: **3 Bc4-e2 check Kh5-h4**.

White's minor pieces have now set up the corridor, with his Bishops guarding g4 and g5, while his Knight guards g7. (The Knight also cuts off the Black Bishop on c8 from helping in the defense – an interference idea.) The Black King is trapped on h4, and the only problem is how to use the remaining pieces that aren't occupied in constructing the corridor to deliver the mate. White finds a neat solution: **4 Rf1-f4 check! Ng6xf4 5 g2-g3 check Kh4-h3 6 Nd5xf4 mate.**

USING THE ROOK IN THE CORRIDOR MATE

Although most corridor mates involve the Queen and the minor pieces, the Rooks can also cooperate under certain circumstances. The problem with using the Rooks is that the h-file corridor is usually blocked from the attacker's end by his own h-pawn. In order for the Rooks to participate, they have to be activated along the third or fourth rank, through a maneuver known as a **Rook lift**.

A Rook lift simply involves moving a Rook from the corner out to one of the open center files, then up to the third or fourth rank. From this position the Rook can swing along the rank, in front of its own pawns, attacking the enemy position. Used this way, the Rook can be an extremely powerful attacking piece.

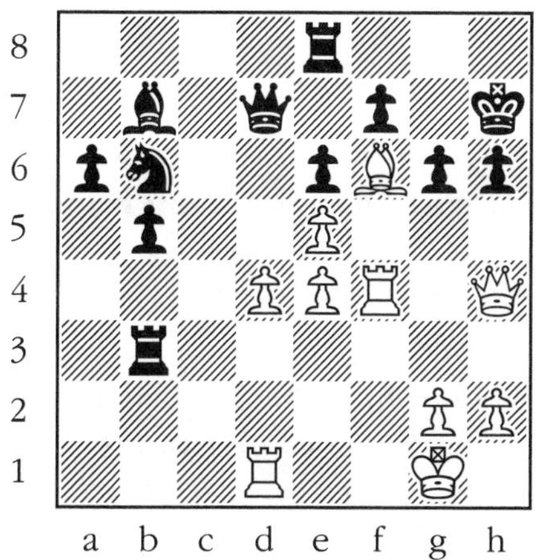

Diagram 86: White on move

Here's a simple example of a Rook lift leading to a winning corridor attack. Earlier in the game, White had swung his Rook from f1 to f4, where it's now ready to move along the fourth rank. Now he can force a corridor mate in just two moves: **1 Qh4xh6 check!** (opening the h-file for the Rook) **Kh7xh6 2 Rf4-h4 mate**.

The Rook is so powerful that corridor mates with a Rook assisting are usually much simpler to calculate than attacks with Knights and Bishops.

Here are a couple of more examples.

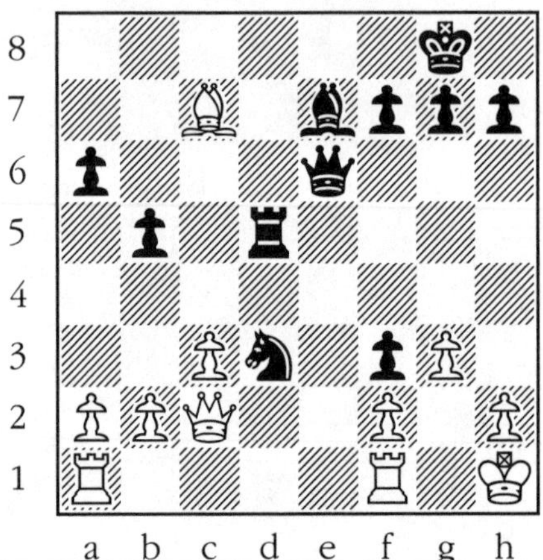

Diagram 87: Black on move

In Diagram 87 Black has the makings of a strong attack, since his f-pawn has managed to penetrate to f3, weakening the White King-side. In addition, Black has managed to lift his Rook to the fourth rank, ready to move over to the King-side. Black now sees a forced mate, based on a corridor mate on the h-file.

He starts with **1 ... Qe6-h3**, threatening mate at g2. White has only one defense, so he plays **2 Rf1-g1**, guarding g2.

Now Black finishes nicely: **2 ... Qh3xh2 check! 3 Kh1xh2 Rd5-h5 mate**. The Rook lift to the fourth rank provided the necessary firepower for mate along the h-file.

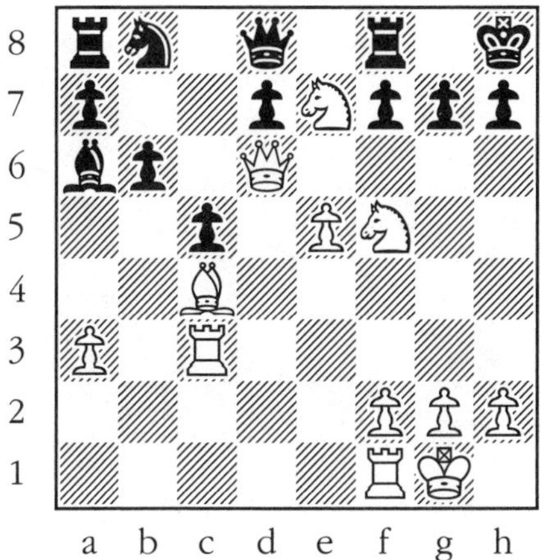

Diagram 88: White on move

In Diagram 88 White has a tremendous position, but what's the best way to win? He's managed to lift his Queen's Rook from a1 to c3, so the Rook can now operate along the whole open third rank. Watch as White uses the power of the corridor mate to force a beautiful finish.

White starts with a move that looks like a typographical misprint: **1 Qd6-g6!!** This amazing move threatens mate at g7 next turn, so Black needs to take the Queen. He sees that if he plays 1 ... h7xg6, White will just play 2 Rc3-h3 mate. So he takes with the other pawn: **1 ... f7xg6**. Now White finishes with **2 Ne7xg6 check! h7xg6 3 Rc1-h3 check Qd8-h4 4 Rh3xh4 mate**. When the Black f-pawn moved, it opened the diagonal from c4 to g8 for the White Bishop.

This kept the Black King pinned in the corner, so he was doomed as soon as the h-file could be pried open.

11

MATES USING THE LONG DIAGONAL

A Bishop located on the long diagonal aiming at the enemy King is an extremely powerful attacking piece. If the pawn on g7 can be knocked out of position, the Bishop becomes a dagger aimed at the Black King, controlling the f6, g7, and h8 squares. With the addition of just one other piece, usually a Knight or a Rook, a variety of checkmating patterns are possible.

THE FIVE BASIC PATTERNS

The next five diagrams show the five basic checkmating patterns utilizing a Bishop on the long diagonal.

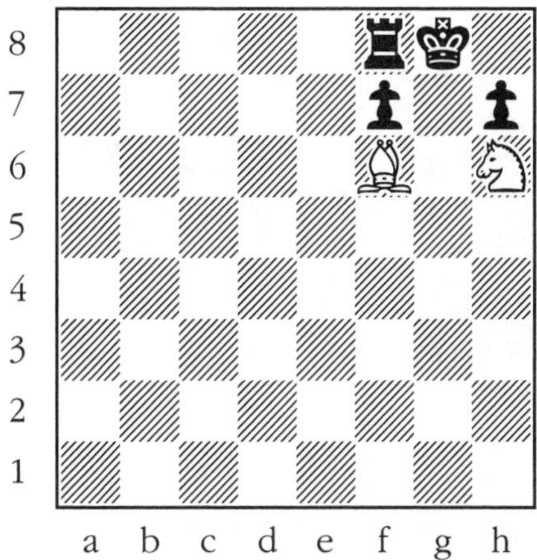

Diagram 89: Pattern #1: Bishop plus Knight

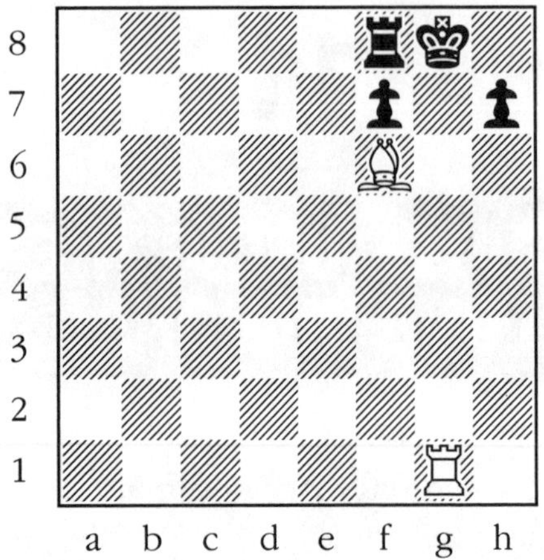

Diagram 90: Pattern #2: Bishop plus Rook

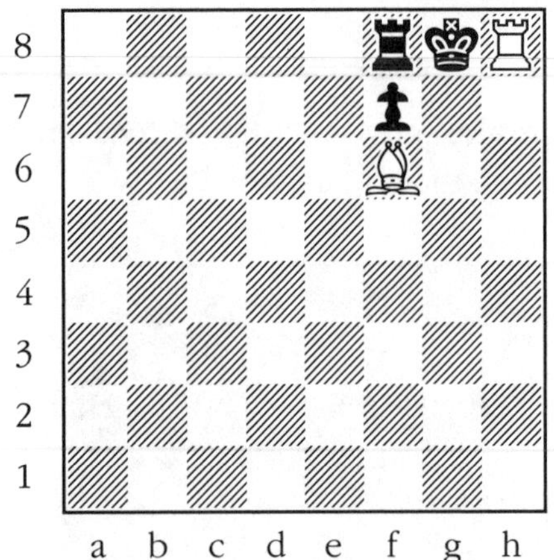

Diagram 91: Pattern #3: Bishop plus Rook

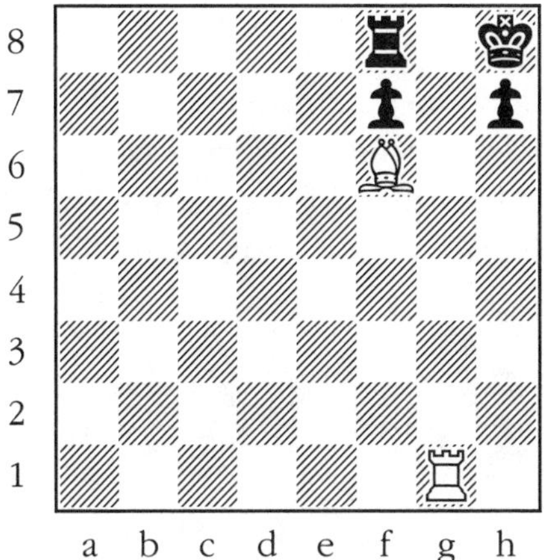

Diagram 92: Pattern #4: Rook plus Bishop

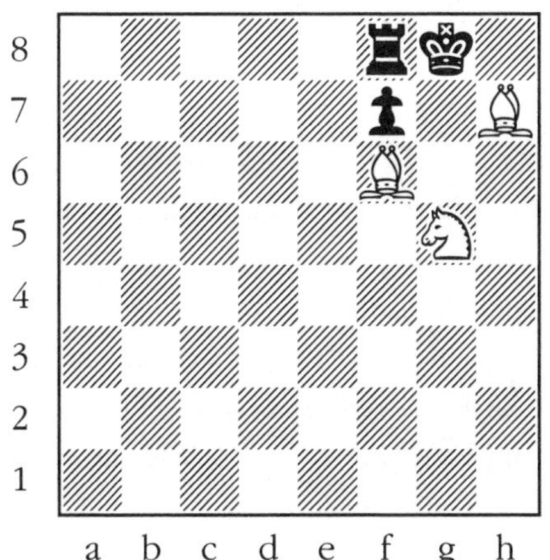

Diagram 93: Pattern #5: Bishop plus two minor pieces

To make the long diagonal attack work, the King's defenses must first be weakened in some way. All require the pawn on g7 to be moved. Pattern #2 and #4 require the g-file to be completely open. Pattern #3 requires the h-file open. If the Rook isn't involved, a mate can be effected even with all files closed; that's the idea of Pattern #1.

The first part of a successful long-diagonal attack involves weakening the King's defending pawn structure; the second part involves breaking through for the final checkmate. Now let's look at some real examples using these different patterns.

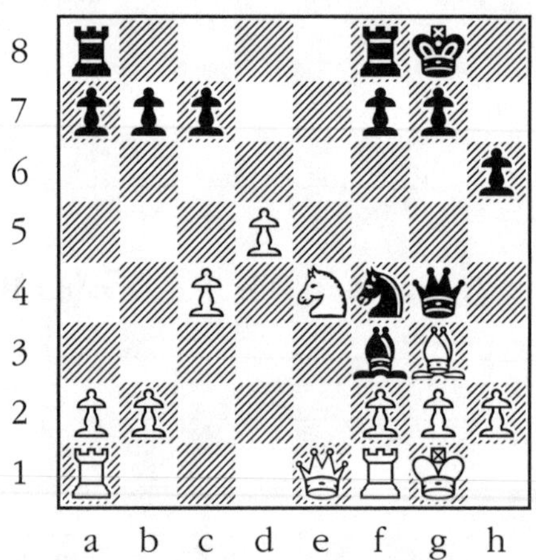

Diagram 94: Black on move

Normally a successful mating attack hinges on having more pieces on the attack than your opponent can muster for the defense. In Diagram 94, White seems to be doing quite well on the defense. He has four pieces defending his King, while Black only has three for his attack.

White's problem is that Black's pieces are all aimed at the one weak point in White's position, a point that White can't defend at all – the g2 square. Black's winning combination simply piles more force on that weak spot. He plays **1 ... Qg4-h3!!**

Black threatens to capture on g2 with mate, so White must take off the Queen: **2 g2xh3**. Black finishes the game with **2 ... Nf4xh3 mate** – an example of mating pattern #1.

Here's a longer example of that same pattern:

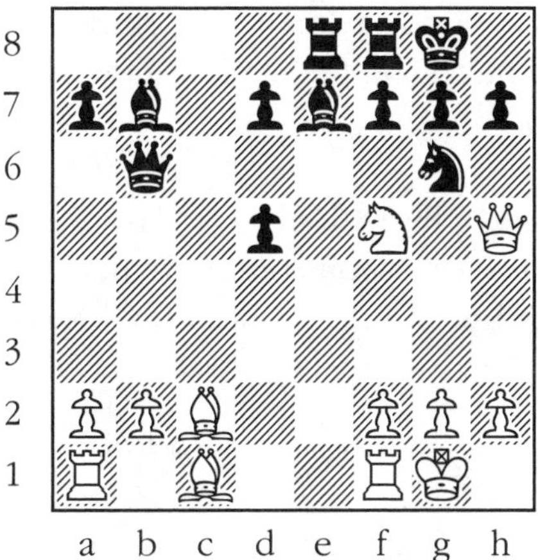

Diagram 95: White on move

White's pieces are clearly posted well in Diagram 95, but no immediate win is clear. White's immediate problem is the development of his Queen's Bishop. He'd like to get it into the game, but right now it's tied down to the defense of the b-pawn. What should White do?

An unimaginative player might try a slow, safe development with b2-b3 and Bc1-b2. This line of play, however, gives Black time to organize an impregnable defense. However, White was familiar with the basic mating patterns, so he saw a much better line of development.

White started with **1 Bc1-e3!** He's willing to sacrifice the b-pawn to get his Bishop to the long diagonal, because he sees the possibility for a pattern #1 mate. Black, not seeing the possibility, grabbed the b-pawn, **1 ... Qb6xb2**. Now White centralized his Bishop with **2 Be3-d4!**, sacrificing his other Bishop.

Black, not knowing his mating patterns, snapped up the white-squared Bishop with **2 ... Qb2xc2.** (In fairness to Black, the game couldn't be saved at this point, since White was both threatening the Queen and threatening a forced mate based on pattern #1.)

White then uncorked his real surprise: He played the stunning **3 Qh5-h6!!** With mate looming on g7, Black has to take the Queen, **3 ... g7xh6.** White finishes with **4 Nf5xh6**, the mate of pattern #1.

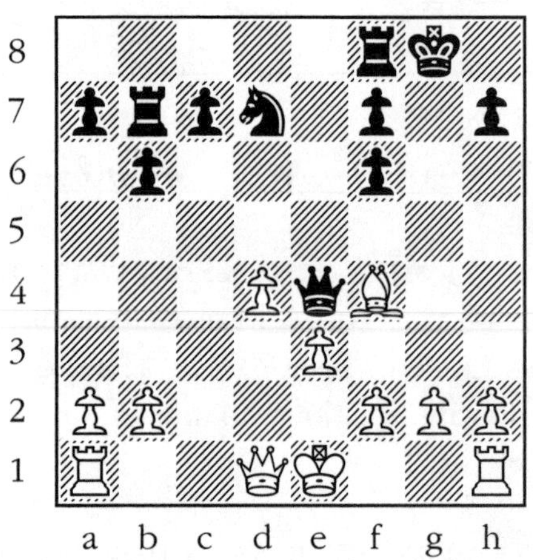

Diagram 96: White on move

It's White's move and Black is attacking the White pawn on g2. A player unfamiliar with the mating patterns of this chapter might simply stop to protect the pawn. White could play 1 0-0, or 1 f2-f3, either of which would guard the g-pawn and give White a small but solid advantage.

White, however, knew his patterns well, in particular pattern #2. Instead of guarding the pawn, he saw that he could sacrifice it for a winning attack. Accordingly, he played **1 Bf4-h6!** The Bishop attacks the Black Rook, but Black didn't see any reason to be concerned. After all, if he takes the g-pawn, he'll be attacking White's undefended Rook. So he played **1 ... Qe4xg2**. "If White takes my Rook, I'll take his," Black reasons.

But White has no intention of taking the Black Rook. The Bishop, controlling the g7 square, is too valuable for that. Instead, White protects his Rook by sacrificing his Queen! He plays **2 Qd1-f3!!**

This is an amazing move to someone unfamiliar with the basic patterns, but routine once you understand them. The White Queen defends the White Rook and, in addition, forks the Black Queen and the Black Rook down at b7. If Black doesn't capture, he has to resign. Sensing something bad coming, Black plays **2 ... Qg2xf3.**

White now ends the game by forcing the mate of pattern #2. He plays **3 Rh1-g1 check Kg8-h8 4 Bh6-g7 check Kh8-g8 5 Bg7xf6 discovered check Qf3-g4 5 Rg1xg4 mate.** Since White knew this pattern was possible once the g-file was opened, the whole startling combination seemed clear to him from the beginning.

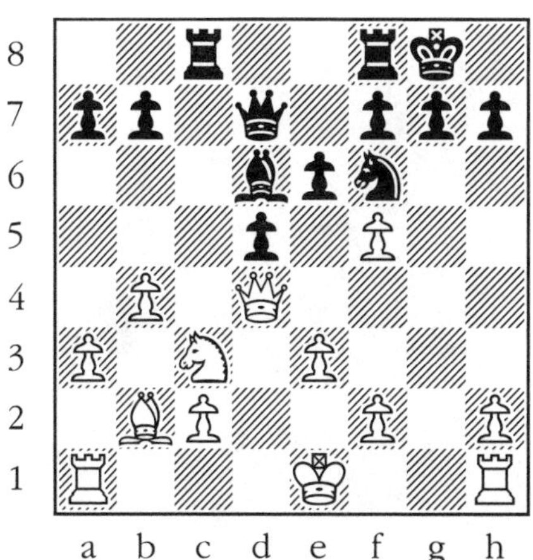

Diagram 97: White on move

White sees the basic elements of pattern #2 in this position: The open g-file leading to Black's King, and the White Bishop on the long diagonal from b2 to g7. Question: can he put these elements together to construct a mating attack? After some thought, White realizes the answer is "yes!".

CLEARANCE SACRIFICES

White starts with the surprise move **1 Nc3xd5!** This is what's known as a clearance sacrifice. White's not interested in winning the d-pawn – the idea is to clear the way for the Bishop on b2 to act on the long diagonal, with no loss of time. You might ask, Why not just play 1 Nc3-e2? Wouldn't that clear the diagonal just as well without sacrificing anything? The answer is no. Because moving to e2 wouldn't involve a threat, Black would have time to defend; he'd just play 1 ... e6-e5, and his position would be safe.

Black naturally plays **1 ... e6xd5**, winning the Knight. Now White shows the real point of his play. He moves **2 Qd4xf6!**, ripping open the g-file. After **2 ... g7xf6**, White mates with **3 Rh1-g1 check Kg8-h8 4 Bb2xf6 mate**.

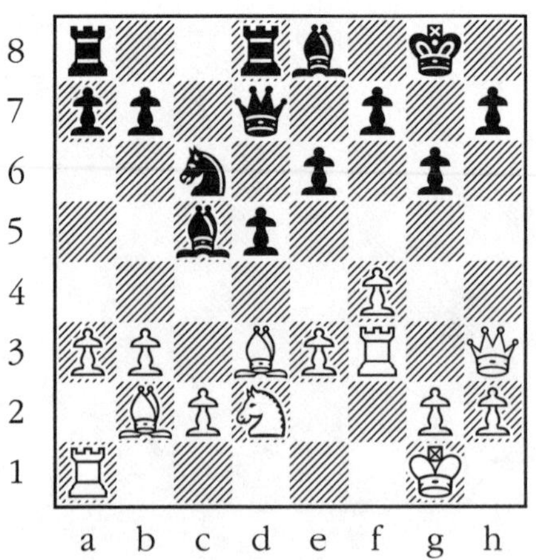

Diagram 98: White on move

Diagram 98 has the basic components for mating pattern #3: a Bishop operating on the long diagonal covering the g7 and h8 squares, and a Rook which has been lifted to the third rank ready to move over to the h-file. All that's necessary is for the h-file to be cleared, and White is able to do that in one stroke with a Queen sacrifice.

He plays **1 Qh3xh7 check!** The idea is to enable his Rook to reach the h3-square with another check, so Black won't have time to block the h-file.

Black plays **1 ... Kg8xh7**, and White finishes with **2 Rf3-h3 check Kh7-g8 3 Rh3-h8 mate**. A perfect example of pattern #3.

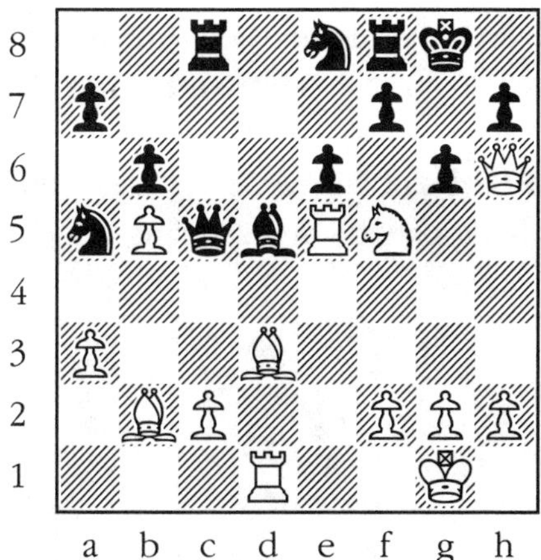

Diagram 99: White on move

Here's another example of pattern #3, in a more complex form. You'll notice some similarities right away. The White Bishop on b2 operates on the long diagonal, as before. And White has lifted his Rook to e5, where it could swing over to the h-file. Also, the White Queen is in position to open the h-file with a sacrifice, just as in the last problem.

But there are a few key differences as well. The Bishop is blocked from attacking g7 and g8 by the Rook on e5, which will have to move to get the Bishop into play. The Rook is prevented from reaching h5, its target spot on the h-file, by the Knight at f5. And even if the Rook gets to h5, it's subject to being captured by the Black pawn. Can White untangle all these threads?

Yes he can, if he makes his moves in the proper order. Here's how it's done. White starts with a Knight sacrifice: **1 Nf5-e7 check!** This is another clearance sacrifice – the Knight gets out of the way of the Rook, and loses no time by giving a check.

Black captures, **1 ... Qc5xe7.** Now White makes another sacrifice, this time to open the h-file: **2 Qh6xh7 check! Kg8xh7**. Now the road is cleared for the Rook, but with a bonus. The Knight's move cleared the way for the White Bishop on d3, which now pins the pawn on g6! So White can play **3 Re5-h5 check**, and Black can't capture because of the pin. He has to fall into **3 ... Kh7-g8 4 Rh5-h8 mate**. That was a nice example of seeing the underlying pattern and steering directly toward it.

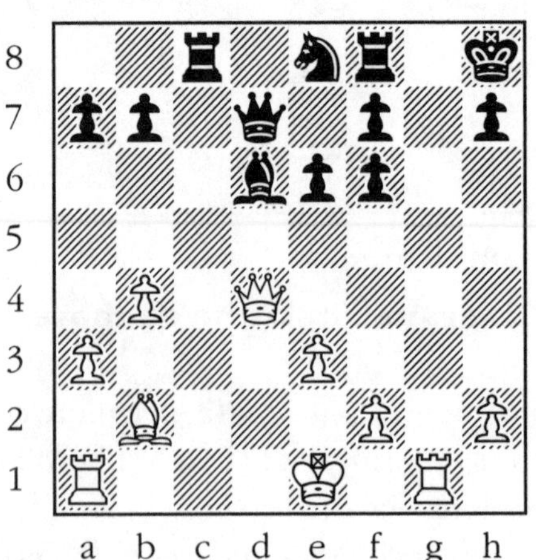

Diagram 100: White on move

Mating pattern #4 isn't quite as common as some of the others. Diagram 100 shows a short example. White's Rook already controls the open g-file, and his Bishop and Queen are lined up on the long diagonal. White has a quick mate in two moves:

1 Qd4xf6 check! Ne8xf6 2 Bb2xf6 mate.

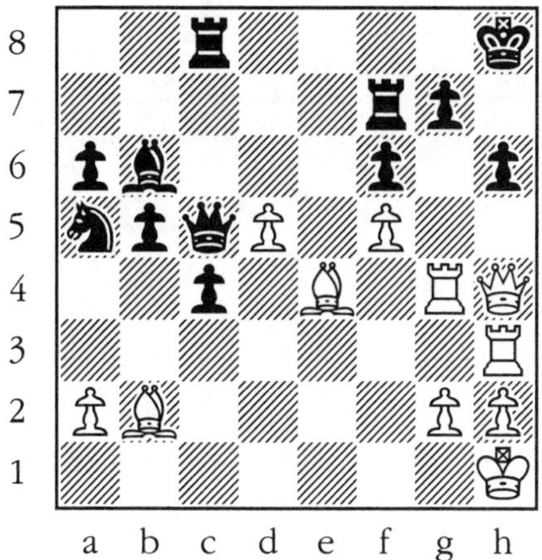

Diagram 101: White on move

Diagram 101 shows the same pattern, but the mate here is more difficult to find. For the mate to work, Black is going to have to be forced to block the h7-square. And White will need to hurry, since Black is also threatening mate at g1 with his Queen.

Fortunately, White's lineup of power on the g- and h-files is just enough to do the job.

White starts with **1 Qh4xh6 check!**, breaking through the pawn barrier on the King-side, and incidentally, opening up the g-file for his Rook to control. Black plays **1 ... g7xh6**, and White continues with **2 Rh3xh6 check.** With White's Rooks now controlling the two open files, he has no choice: **2 ... Rf7-h7**.

With the Black King now immobilized, White finishes with **3 Bb2xf6 mate**. The King was helpless once the defending phalanx of pawns was blasted away.

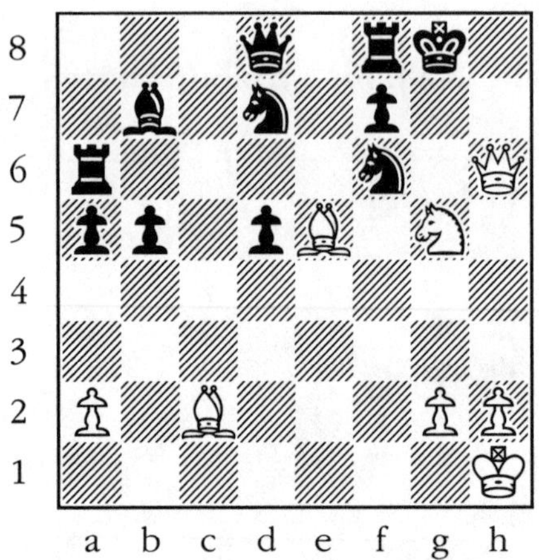

Diagram 102: White on move

Without a knowledge of mating pattern #5, White seems to have a strong attack but no square on which to actually force a mate. For instance, 1 Bc2-h7 check Kg8-h8 2 Bh7-c2 discovered check Kh8-g8 just leads to a perpetual check.

But with a knowledge of the mating patterns, checkmate is quite easy: White just plays **1 Qh6-h7 check! Nf6xh7 2 Bc2xh7 mate.**

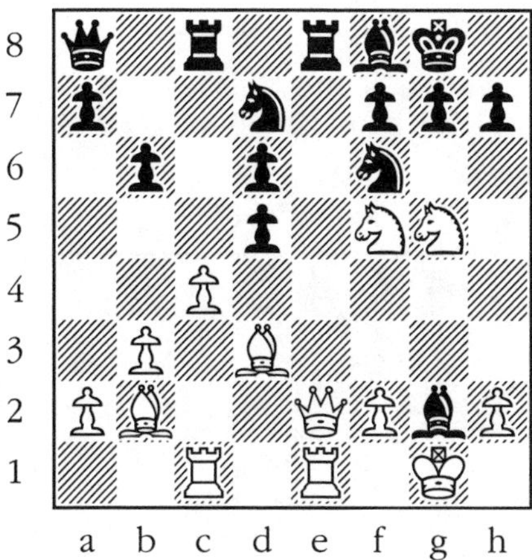

Diagram 103: White on move

In Diagram 103, Black has just played Be7-f8, guarding g7 and uncovering an attack on the White Queen by the Rook on e8. If White retreats, his attack will grind to a halt. Remembering mating pattern #5, however, lets White see his way to a mating attack with a brilliant sacrifice.

White plays **1 Qe2-h5!!** He threatens mate in three moves by the sequence: 2 Nf5-h6 check g7xh6 3 Qh5xf7 check Kg8-h8 4 Qf7xh7 mate. (The Knight on f6 would be pinned by the Bishop on b2.) Black doesn't have a good defense, so he takes the Queen: **1 ... Nf6xh5**. Now White uncorks **2 Nf5-h6 check! g7xh6 3 Bd3xh7 mate**. By clearing out the Knights on f5 and f6, pattern #5 was possible.

BEYOND THE BASIC PATTERNS

The attacking Bishop on the long diagonal leading to the enemy King is such a potent attacking force that many different mating formations are possible. The five patterns listed at the beginning of this chapter are the major formations to remember. However, any time you can set up an attacking Bishop on the long diagonal, you should check out the available captures and checks around the King to see if a checkmate is possible.

The next few problems show some unusual but potent attacks which don't fit any of the major patterns.

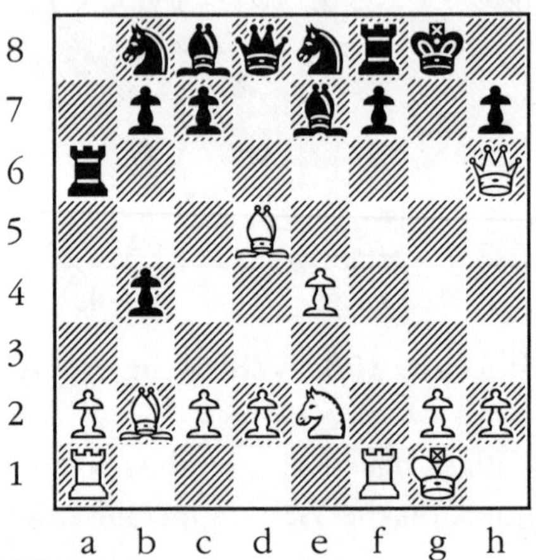

Diagram 104: White on move

In Diagram 104, White has sacrificed a Knight to open up the files and diagonals leading to the Black King. Although Black's pieces are confined to the first two rows, they seem to be guarding most of the vital squares. The Knight at e8 is stopping any mate at g7. The Bishop at e7 prevents any attacks via f6 or g5.

In addition, Black has just lifted his Queen's Rook to a6, where it attacks the White Queen. If White retreats the Queen, Black's Rook can swing over to g6, where his position will be very secure.

If White wants to win, he will have to win quickly. But where's the win? White finds it, based on the strength of the Bishop at b2 coupled with the awesome power of a double check (or two).

White starts with **1 Qh6xf8 check!!** Most unexpected. Black has to reply **1 ... Kg8xf8.** Now White plays **2 Rf1xf7 check**, and Black has to move **2 ... Kf8-g8**.

Now White reveals the real point of his play. He moves **3 Rf7-g7 double check!** Both the Bishop at d5 and the Rook at g7 are under attack, but since it's a double check, Black can only get out of check by moving his King: **3 ... Kg8-h8**. White finishes his attack with **4 Rg7-g8 double check and mate!** Black's King is under attack from both the Rook on g8 and the Bishop on b2.

The Rook is protected by the Bishop on d5, so there's no safe place to move the King. Game over.

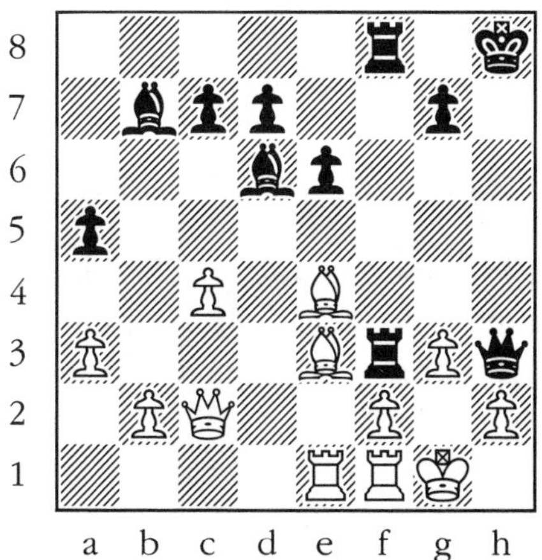

Diagram 105: Black on move

Black has the makings of a strong attack in Diagram 105, with a Bishop on the long diagonal, two powerful Rooks on the f-file, and a menacing Queen strongly posted at h3. Still White's defenses look adequate. The f- and g-pawns are bulwarks of strength, and White's last move, Bd3-e4, looks like it will succeed in trading off the Black Bishop at b7 after which Black's attacking chances should be much reduced. Can Black break through?

The weak point in White's position appears to be the pawn at h2. If Black could maneuver a Rook over to the h-file, say to h5, then he'd have an unstoppable threat of mate at h2.

But how can a Rook get there? The White Bishops control f4, f5, g6, and h6, seemingly controlling all the approach routes to the h-file.

Black has a way to break through, however, based on the insight that one of White's pieces is overworked, needing to perform two critical defensive jobs. Can you spot the overworked pieces? Black's first move should give you a clue. He plays **1 ... Rf8-f5!!** His idea is to ignore the White Bishop guarding f5 and just play the Rook over to h5 for a quick checkmate. Having no real choice, White snaps off the Rook with **2 Be4xf5**, expecting Black to recapture.

But Black doesn't recapture. Instead, he plays a move more amazing than his previous: **2 ... Qh3-g2 check!!** Very nice, but isn't the Queen a little ... unprotected? White gobbles it up, **3 Kg1xg2.**

And now comes the punch line: Black plays **3 ... Rf3xg3 double check and mate!**

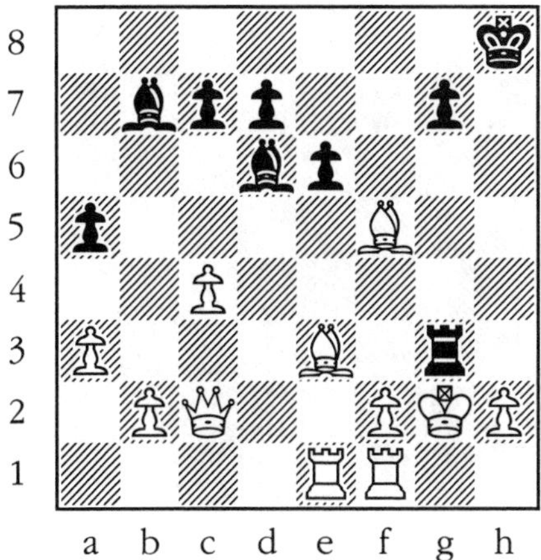

Diagram 106: White is checkmated!

Once again the awesome power of the double check shines through. The White King is attacked by the Bishop at b7 and the Rook at g3. The only response to a double check is to move the King, but f3, h3, g1, and h1 are all under attack, and the Rook is guarded by the Bishop at d6. It's over.

The key to this combination was the overworked White Bishop on e4. It not only had to stop the Black Rook from swinging over to h5 via f5, but also to block the action of the Black Bishop from b7.

That was one job too many.

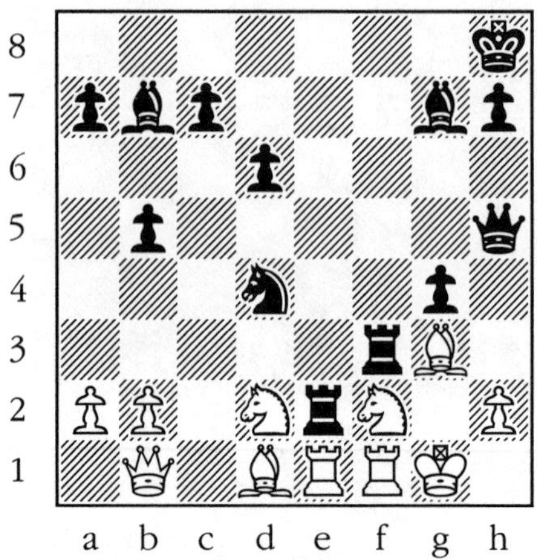

Diagram 107: Black on move

Once again Black has a strong attacking formation, and the Black Bishop on the long diagonal looks menacing. Black finds the breakthrough with two bold strokes, leading to a mate at g2.

He starts with **1 ... Rf3xg3 check!** This opens the long diagonal for the Bishop on b7. White recaptures, **2 h2xg3**.

Next comes **2 ... Qh5-h1 check!!** This opens the second rank for the Rook on e2. White plays **3 Nf2xh1**, and Black finishes with **3 ... Re2-g2 mate**. The King is boxed in by his own pieces, and the combination of the Rook plus the Bishop on b7 was enough for mate.

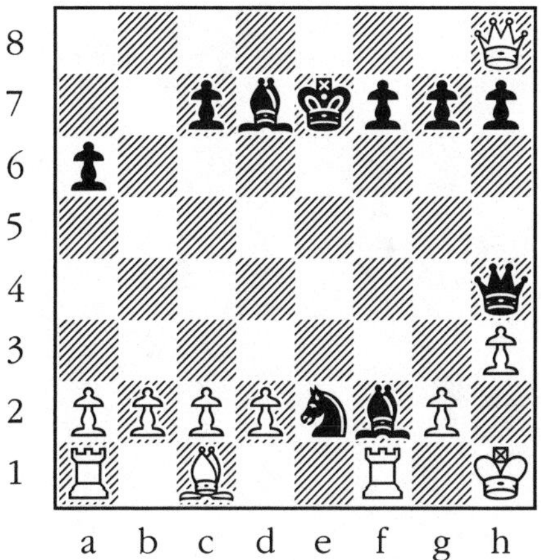

Diagram 108: Black on move

The entire middle of the board is empty in Diagram 108, giving Black's Bishops plenty of room to operate. The result is a mate which is a close relative of mating pattern #5.

Black starts with a Queen sacrifice: **1 ... Qh4xh3 check!** White has no choice, **2 g2xh3.**

Black finishes by repositioning his Bishops, **2 ... Bd7-c6 check 3 Kh1-h2 Bf2-g3 mate**.

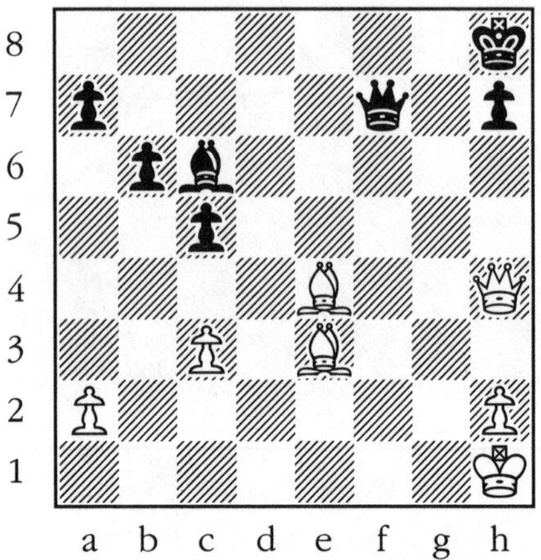

Diagram 109: Black on move

At first glance there doesn't appear to be enough material left in Diagram 109 to force a checkmate. White's King has plenty of elbow room, his Bishops control all the approaches to the King, Black's long diagonal Bishop is neutralized by the White Bishop, and, not least, White is a piece ahead. Can Black forge a mating attack out of this unpromising beginning?

Black starts with **1 ... Qf7-f1 check**. "No problem," thinks White. "I had that check covered." He blocks with **2 Be3-g1**, expecting Black to resign.

Instead of resigning, Black announces checkmate in two moves! White still doesn't see it, but Black shows him what he had overlooked: **2 ... Qf1-f3 check!! 3 Be4xf3 Bc6xf3 mate**. Black's first move took away the King's escape squares, so a check on the diagonal was all that was needed.

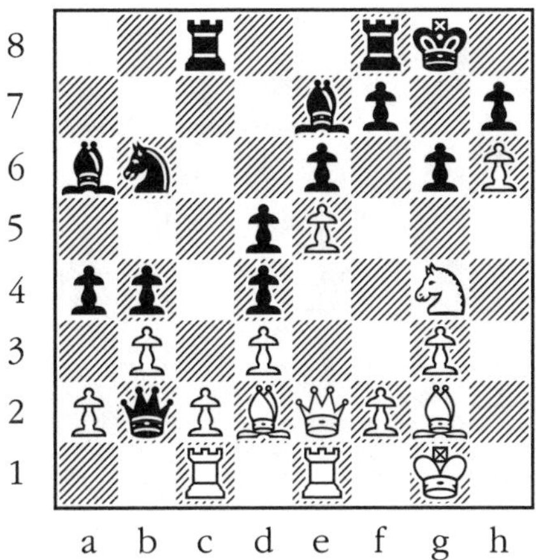

Diagram 110: White on move

Diagram 110 shows a nice combination from one of my own games played some years ago. Material is even but Black's Queen has penetrated to the b2-square, and it looks like White is going to lose either the c2-pawn or the a2-pawn. However, I saw the possibility for a nice trap.

My first move was **1 Qe2-f3!** This seems to abandon the c2-pawn to Black. It's also not clear just what is being threatened on the King-side. It would be nice to play Qf3-f6-g7 mate, but the Black Bishop halts that plan. I could play my Knight to f6 check, but the Black King just hides in the corner.

I can't trade off the Black Bishop with Bd2-g5, since Black could just capture me there.

Seeing no threat either, Black grabs the c-pawn, **1 ... Rc8xc2.** I trade the Rooks, **2 Rc1xc2 Qb2xc2**.

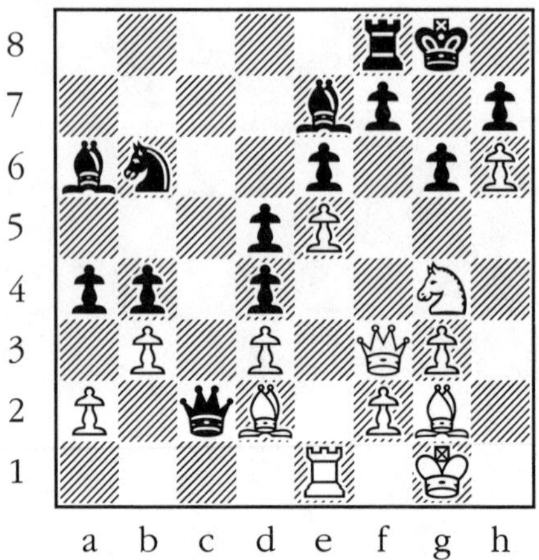

Diagram 111: White on move

Now what? My pawn at d3 is about to go, and I'm still not threatening anything. Or am I? My next move gets the pawn back: **3 Bd2xb4!** The first sign of trouble. Black can't recapture, since I'd play Qf3-f6 and mate at g7. Instead, Black has to retreat to protect the Bishop at e7: **3 ... Qc2-c7**.

Black still looks okay since he can recapture with the Queen if I exchange Bishops and still guard the vital f6 square. But my next move was the real surprise since keeping me out of f6 is harder than it looks. I played **4 Qf3-f6!**

The threat is mate at g7, so Black has to capture: **4 ... Be7xf6**. But then, amazingly, mate comes at f7 anyway. The final sequence was **5 Ng4xf6 check Kg8-h8 6 Bb4xf8 and 7 Bf8-g7 mate.** Mate on the long diagonal after all!

The loser of this game, by the way, was Dan Harrington, who went on to become the 1995 World Champion of Poker.

12

MATE WITH TWO BISHOPS

Under the right circumstances, two Bishops by themselves can administer a checkmate. Usually the enemy King will have to be seriously impeded by his own pieces for this attack to work.

There are two different mating patterns for the two Bishops: the crisscross and the battery. In actual play, the crisscross is more common, and it's one of the few mating patterns that works well against Queen-side castling. Here are samples of the two basic patterns:

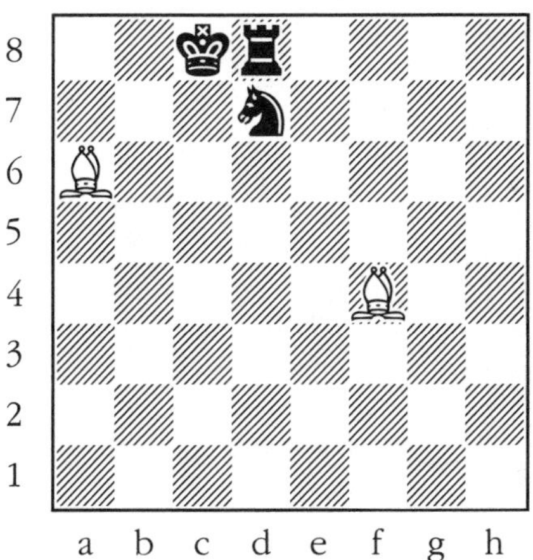

Diagram 112: Pattern #1: the crisscross

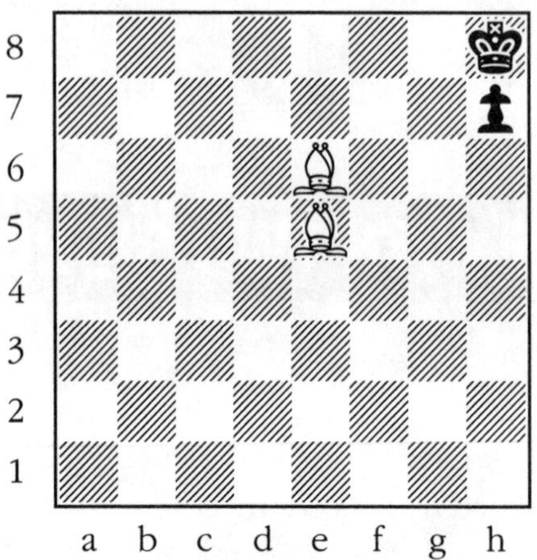

Diagram 113: Pattern #2: the battery

In the crisscross, the Black King is blocked on one side by his Rook and Knight. The Bishop on f4 is able to guard two escape squares, while the other Bishop checks and guards the final square. The battery is a simpler formation, but it wouldn't work if the Black pawns weren't an obstruction at h7.

Now let's look at some real-life examples. We'll start with the crisscross pattern.

THE CRISSCROSS

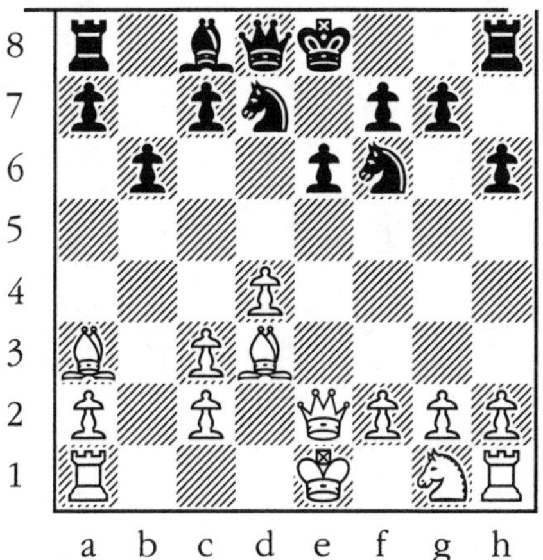

Diagram 114: White on move

Diagram 114 shows a mating assault right out of the opening. Black seems perfectly well-developed; the only apparent flaw in his game is his inability to castle King-side because of the White Bishop at a3.

However, that Bishop is actually a dreadful attacking force, as White's next move proves: **1 Qe2xe6 check!! f7xe6 2 Bd3-g6 mate!**

This is a good combination to remember, as it can arise from a number of different openings; the key is that Black's dark-squared Bishop is no longer defending the diagonal next to Black's King.

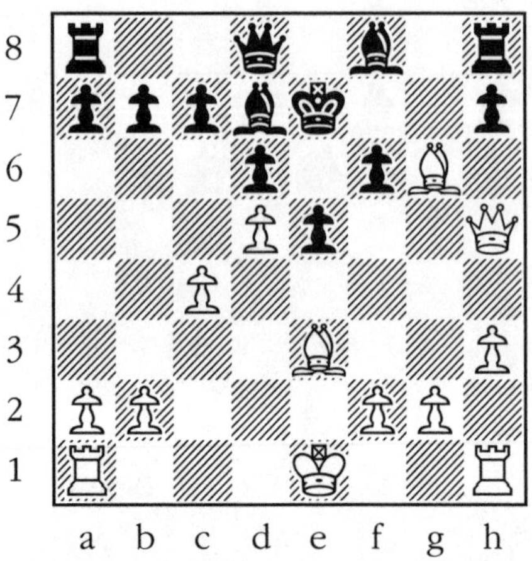

Diagram 115: White on move

Diagram 115 is an especially nice demonstration of the power of the Bishops. White is off to a nice start, with Black's King misplaced and his pieces in each other's way. An unimaginative White player might settle for the win of a pawn by Bg6xh7.

But an imaginative player would just announce mate in two moves, starting with **1 Qh5xe5 check!!** If Black plays 1 ... f6xe5, White has 2 Be3-g5 mate. If Black tries 1 ... d6xe5, White has a mirror-image finish: 2 Be3-c5 mate.

Very elegant.

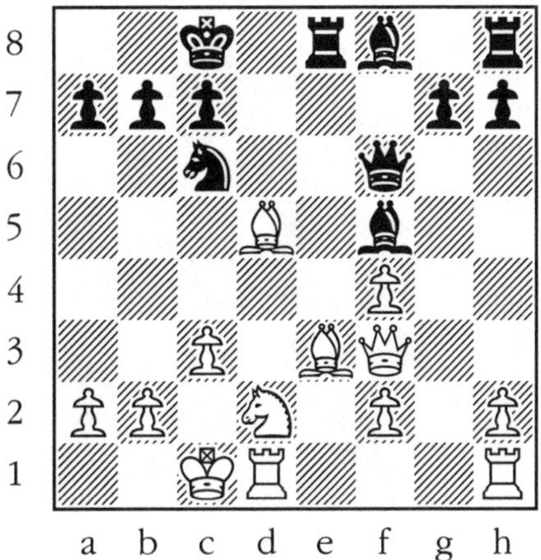

Diagram 116: Black on move

What's particularly deceptive about the Two Bishop's Mate is that, since the Bishops are long-range pieces, it can arise out of seemingly unthreatening positions.

Take Diagram 116. Black is a pawn down and no piece has even penetrated to White's half of the board.

No matter. "Lights out!", says Black, as he plays **1 ... Qf6xc3 check!! 2 b2xc3 Bf8-a3 mate.** A good example of the power of the attack against a Queen-side castled position, once a Bishop has been established on the b1-f5 diagonal.

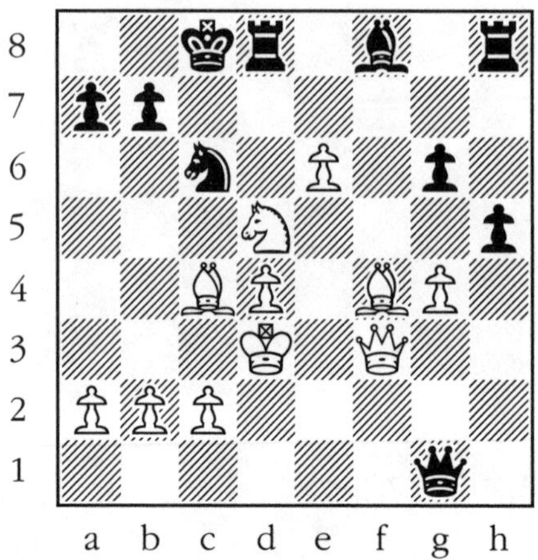

Diagram 117: White on move

The key elements of the Queen-side attack with the two Bishops are: (1) the King blocked from the d7 and d8 squares, and; (2) a Bishop on the f4-b8 diagonal. Here both elements are in place since the pawn at e6 keeps the Black King pinned in place. White just needs to figure out a way to open up the a6-c8 diagonal for his Bishop without losing any time.

Here a couple of clearance moves do the trick: **1 Nd5-b6 check!** (opens up a diagonal for the Queen on f3) **1 ... a7xb6 2 Qf3xc6 check!!** (opens up the vital diagonal) **2 ... b7xc6 3 Bc4-a6 mate**. Easy when you know how.

THE BATTERY

The battery formation is less common, but works well when the enemy King is trapped in the corner. It can even work against a King in the center, provided the King's own pieces get in the way.

Diagram 118 is a case in point.

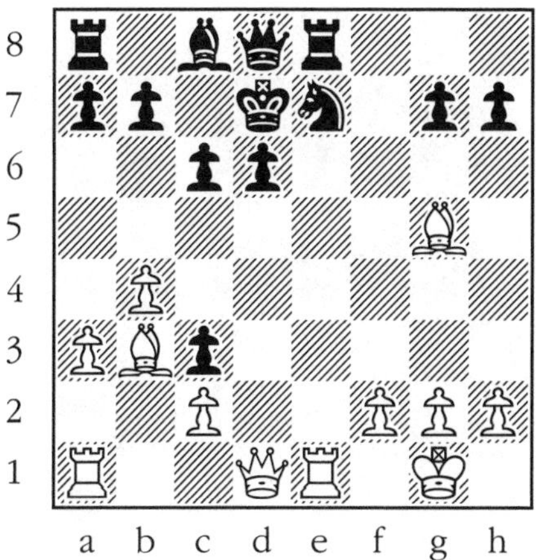

Diagram 118: White on move

Black's King is trapped in the center and he's hanging on by a thread. White breaks through with his Queen, then uses the Bishops to set up a battery: **1 Qd1xd6 check!! Kd7xd6 2 Bg5-f4 check! Kd6-d7 3 Bb3-e6 mate**.

With Black's pieces blocking all escape routes, White's Bishops just needed a little help from his Rook.

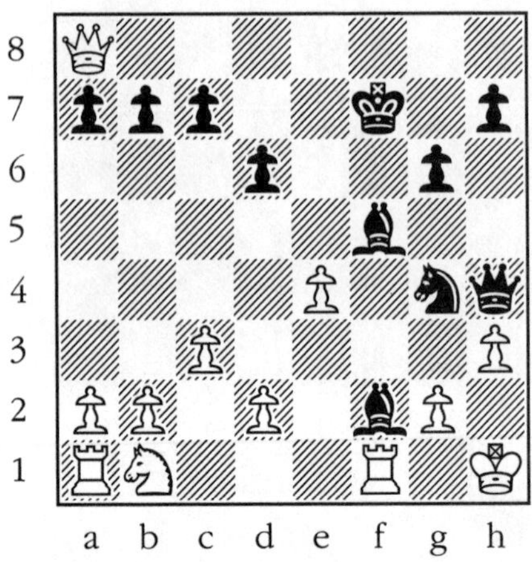

Diagram 119: Black on move

With the King trapped in the corner, White has little enough mobility to make a battery possible. Black wins with **1 ... Qh4xh3 check! 2 g2xh3 Bf5xe4 mate.**

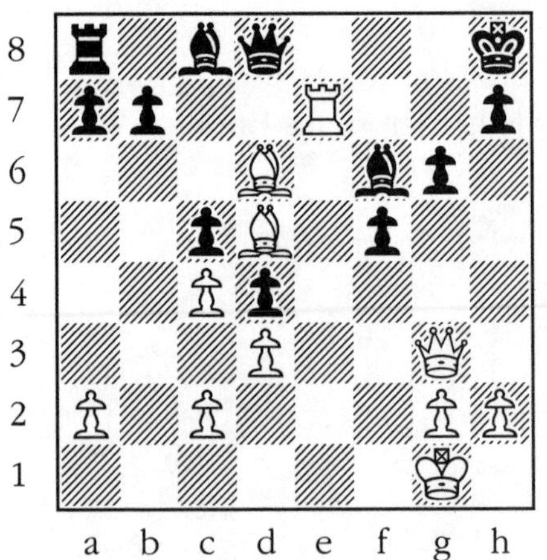

Diagram 120: White on move

White's pieces are all in position to make something happen. The Black King is trapped in the corner and his only active piece is the Bishop on f6. White has more than one way to win, but the most elegant is **1 Qg3-h4!!** White threatens both 2 Qh4xf6 mate and 2 Qh4xh7 mate, so Black must capture, walking into a battery mate: **1 ... Bf6xh4 2 Bd6-e5 check! Bh4-f6 3 Be5xf6 mate.**

13

NEXT STEPS

You've now completed our introduction to the strategy and tactics of checkmating attacks. If you're like most players, you should find that this knowledge will make a tremendous difference in your games. With the patterns of checkmating attacks clearly in mind, you'll be able to spot opportunities in your games that would have passed you by before. Not only will you see actual checkmates when they arise, you'll be alert for chances to weaken your opponent's King position, so that mating attacks might be possible at a later stage.

Of course, it's easier to launch a checkmating attack if you have more material than your opponent. Be sure to read "Winning Chess Tactics", another book in the Road to Chess Mastery series, to understand the various tactical combinations that will help you win material at all stages of the game.

You'll also want to make sure that you have plenty of opponents to play. Besides your own circle of friends, it's important to play against a wide variety of different players and styles. You'll learn faster that way, and your games will become more interesting and more dynamic. The book "Beginning Chess Play" explains how to find clubs and tournaments in your area.

Keep reading, keep playing, and keep winning!